YOUTH ON THE
SANTA FE TRAIL

Camilla Kattell

Light Horse Publishing
Santa Fe, New Mexico

Youth on the Santa Fe Trail
By Camilla Kattell

Light Horse Publishing
Santa Fe, New Mexico
www.lighthorsepublishing.com

ISBN 9780996675406

Library of Congress Control Number: 2015912734

Map image courtesy of Fray Angelico Chavez History Library

Cover and interior design by Andrew and Mary Neighbour, MediaNeighbours.com

Printed in the United States of America

First Edition

Dedicated to those who sustain me:
Chris, Trish, Doug, Sam, and Jake

CONTENTS

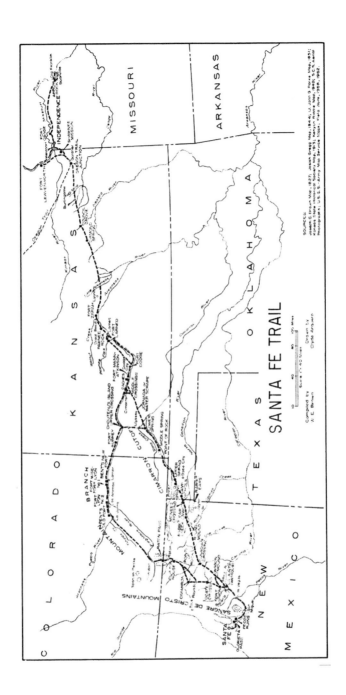

FOREWORD

THE SANTA FE TRAIL, from 1821 to 1880, was an overland route of commerce, with caravans of travelers and freight wagons moving back and forth between Missouri and New Mexico. Secondarily, it was a military road, followed by General Stephen Watts Kearny's Army of the West and other troops to take control of the Southwest during the war with Mexico (1846–1848), after which military posts were established to protect travelers from American Indians, with troops and supply wagons going to and returning from field campaigns and forts along the route and in the American Southwest. Those heading to the gold fields of California and the Rocky Mountains also used the trail. The fascinating history and the network of routes traveled have captured the interest and imagination of generations of Americans.

While hundreds of books and articles have been written about the Santa Fe Trail, few of those are directed to young people. Books about the trail written for children and young adults are mostly fiction and activity books. Camilla Kattell has filled an important niche in trail literature with these true stories of adventure, romance, hard work, and freedom. These biographies of young trail travelers will delight readers young and old. Kattell understands that today's young readers will be able to identify most readily with the stories of young women and men who traveled the Santa Fe Trail. This is the best way to introduce the study of history to the next generation.

It is a pleasure to read about young Kit Carson running away from his apprenticeship as a saddle maker in Missouri to join a wagon train on the Santa Fe Trail and discover that the master from whom he escaped offered a reward of one cent to anyone who returned the apprentice. Carson witnessed the amputation of the gun-shot arm of a fellow traveler on the prairie, where there was no surgeon and no medical equipment. His later career as mountain man, army scout, soldier, and Indian agent is legendary.

The memoir of Marion Sloan Russell, who traveled the trail five times, beginning at age seven, is an American classic, as is the diary of Susan Shelby Magoffin. This teenage bride of a trail merchant accompanied the caravan in 1846, the first year of the Mexican-American War, and followed the Army of the West to Santa Fe and beyond. Their stories are told here, and many readers will be inspired to read Marion's memoir and Susan's diary.

The same is true regarding the accounts of Hector Lewis Garrard and William B. Napton, both of whom set forth on the trail at age seventeen, and the writings of Josiah Gregg, Francis Parkman Jr., and James Ross Larkin. The tall tales of "Uncle Dick" Wootton will challenge readers to seek understanding of what is true and what is "just a good story." The poignant account of José Librado Gurulé, a young New Mexican who traveled the trail to Missouri and back, earned a total of $8 for his hard work, and returned with the first store-bought suit in his hometown (of which he remained proud some seventy years later), provides a Hispanic viewpoint often left out of Santa Fe Trail literature.

Camilla Kattell provides finely crafted biographies, each of which stands alone, that serve as a fascinating introduction to Santa Fe Trail history and will entice readers to want to know more. This collection is highly recommended to readers of all ages.

Leo E. Oliva, Santa Fe Trail
historian, author, and teacher

1

THE SANTA FE TRAIL
ON THE TRAIL OF EXPLORATION

EACH OF US, WHENEVER we are born, arrives on the scene of a long, ongoing story. We have arrived in history. People tend to think of their own time as the only time of significance, not realizing that we are merely temporary actors on the stage of time. We have to read history, talk to older people, study artifacts, or study geology to find the stories of the past and think about their relevance to us. To do so is to know that a girl or boy or even an adult of the past had the same feelings that we have; that we are kindred souls. To learn about how they handled their lives and opportunities can give us feelings of satisfaction in our own choices or goals. It can give us a feeling of continuity.

In the early years of the settlement of the United States, the colonists of the Eastern seaboard gradually made their way west over the Alleghany Mountains to build homes in the forests of the Northwest Territory. The frontier of civilization, as they thought of it, was a dynamic boundary. When settlement reached the Mississippi River and beyond, the forests of the East ended and the plains began. This area was called the

Great American Desert and was an unknown, blank area on maps. Here appeared to be an empty land upon which to expand civilization. Restless Americans had sought free land and believed that taking the land from the Indians, the English, the French, or the Spanish was the right of their destiny to settle the continent between the Atlantic and the Pacific Oceans.

This was a dream of Thomas Jefferson when in 1803 he purchased from Emperor Napoleon Bonaparte of France a vast, unexplored (by Europeans) territory known as the Louisiana Purchase. The 1803 Louisiana Purchase was defined as the Mississippi River Basin, but at that time the boundaries of that area were unknown. The boundaries of the Louisiana Purchase later were established by a treaty between the United States and Spain in 1819. Lieutenant Zebulon Montgomery Pike led a small exploring expedition into the region in 1806, was captured by Spanish troops and taken to Santa Fe and Chihuahua in 1807, and published the journal of his expedition in 1810. His journal pointed out the potential for trade between the United States and northern New Spain (New Mexico) and spurred merchants to seek a way to open trade. These efforts were unsuccessful until Mexico won independence from Spain in 1821.

During the earlier history of the Santa Fe Trail it passed through land that was designated by Congress as unorganized territory prior to being divided into states as settlement developed. Eventually the states of Arkansas, Kansas, Iowa, Missouri, Nebraska, and Oklahoma were formed from within the territory. Also parts of Colorado, Louisiana, Minnesota, Montana, New Mexico, North Dakota, South Dakota, Texas, and Wyoming were originally in the territory. Herein, to help clarify various locations, sometimes state names are used even though states weren't yet formed.

When Mexico won its independence from Spain in 1821, the new government changed the Spanish policy of no intercourse or trade with the United States. Spain had maintained closed borders to deter competition in the sale of her products to colonial Mexico. However, both Mexicans and Americans, sensing lucrative business opportunities, desired to trade with each other. This motivated much of the expansion west of the Mississippi River.

In September 1821, William Becknell and five companions set out from Franklin, Missouri, to establish a trade route to Santa Fe, New Mexico, the capital of the northeastern reaches of Mexico. The passage to Santa Fe had been used periodically, but after Becknell, it became established as the Santa Fe Trail and was the principal route for trade and transportation between the

A typical covered wagon for settlers
(Bent's Old Fort National Historic Site)

two countries. There were several alternate routes over the years, and the Santa Fe Trail was a network of trails rather than a single route of passage.

About 1811, fur traders had established a trail from the western edges of the frontier to the rich trapping areas in the northwest, eventually leading to the valleys of Oregon. This route, known as the Oregon Trail, was only passable by foot and horseback until in the mid-1830s, when better roads were developed for wagon transit, enabling settlers to emigrate from the United States to the rich farmlands of Oregon.

Both of these trails, the Santa Fe Trail and the Oregon Trail, had immense significance for the opening of the West. Beaver furs were highly sought after for trade in the East and in Europe. That lucrative market led adventurous men to explore the mountains and discover what this mysterious land provided in natural resources, and they soon began to fill in the gaps on the map.

In the early years of these trails, adventurous young men and women traveled these routes for various reasons. Some simply sought the experience and adventure and returned east to tell about what they saw. Some journeyed west without realizing that they were early builders and founders of a new civilization.

Susan Shelby Magoffin, one of the early women to travel the trail from the United States and the first to write about her experience, accompanied her trader husband to Santa Fe in 1846. She provided us with a feminine point of view in an amazingly detailed account of life on the trail and what Santa Fe was like. She and several others left us with descriptive journals of their experiences that have provided historians with wonderful tales of the West before it was totally changed by the influx of settlers. Still other young travelers' stories come to us through the telling by a second party or simply by their fame in our history.

These young people not only contributed to the richness of our history but also revealed their own courage, resourcefulness, and perseverance as they ventured into the unknown. In some cases, their innate ability to see the big picture of what was happening to the remarkable native inhabitants gives us perspective on what those American Indians were about to suffer. To these youths who left their remarkable stories, we owe a great debt of gratitude. Their adventures and their strength represent the strength of the people who changed this land and built the foundations of the country we know today. They were part of an unstoppable movement that carried both harm and benefit.

Though each of our characters who traveled the Santa Fe Trail was very unique in their personality, motivations, and outcomes, there were also similarities in their experiences. They were survivors of the horrendous thunderstorms that swept the plains, pelting them with rain and sleet and battering them with high winds. They all dealt with the danger or bother of the bugs and snakes. Their stories of how the wagons navigated the many stream and river crossings had parallels, including accidents that occurred. They had similar comments as they discovered the Indian way of life. Several also remarked on the many French Canadian men who worked on the trail and always seemed to be a happy group with a great deal of resilience to hardship.

Our young travelers all related how they loved the freedom to wander this unknown country and marveled at the beauty of this alien and wild land. This freedom was heady, though they also witnessed the sad graves along the trail and understood the risks in wilderness travel. Each knew the fear of the hostile Indians, who were defending their homeland from invasion by white people. The Indians resisted this incursion and feared the destruction of their way of life.

An event that several experienced in some way was the Taos Rebellion of 1847. After General Stephen Watts Kearny and his Army of the West conquered New Mexico for the United States in 1846, he set up a local government before leaving to conquer California. Charles Bent was named Territorial Governor. He was the partner of Ceran St. Vrain, with whom he built Bent's Fort on the Santa Fe Trail, and he was brother to William Bent who operated Bent's Fort. Charles Bent was a friend and traveling partner to several characters in our story.

Some of the local Mexicans and Indians were not as resigned to US authority as General Kearny had thought. They organized a rebellion against the new government, and on the night of January 19, 1847, they attacked Governor Bent as he visited his family in Taos, New Mexico. Governor Bent was brutally murdered, an event witnessed by his wife, Ignacia, his children, and Kit Carson's wife Josefa. After killing many of the white people in Taos, the mob went to Arroyo Hondo, twelve miles from Taos, and killed everyone in an American settlement there. This event had an effect on the lives of Kit Carson (Chapter 2), Dick Wootton (Chapter 4), and Lewis Garrard (Chapter 7). They each were involved in dealing with the rebellion or with its aftereffects.

Bent's Fort was also a location that most travelers encountered on the Santa Fe Trail, and it provided similar experiences for many. Built in 1833 by Charles Bent, William Bent, and Ceran St. Vrain, it was the only major Anglo-American settlement between the Missouri frontier and the Mexican settlements. It was situated in what is now southeastern Colorado on the Arkansas River. Built for trading with the Southern Cheyenne and Arapaho Indians, it also served as a resupply station on the long trail and a place to rest livestock for the continued trip to Santa Fe.

Our Anglo-American adventurers arrived at some time in Santa Fe and described it as a dirty, shabby place. However, some found attributes in the culture of the Mexican people that they had not expected. It was very foreign to these children of the staid East, but the vigor and happiness of the people was intoxicating. Some mentioned a feeling of regret for leaving this colorful place. José Librado Gurulé provides the point of view of a Spanish youth for whom the adventure was a contribution to survival.

Most found the adventure they had sought, and they returned home to harbor memories of excitement and freedom that nurtured them all their lives. Some, like Kit Carson (Chapter 2), Dick Wootton (Chapter 4), and Marion Sloan Russell (Chapter 8), found a home and worked all their lives to help build an empire, as they thought it should be built. Others, like Lewis Garrard (Chapter 7) and Francis Parkman Jr. (Chapter 5), foresaw the sad demise of the culture of the American Indians and wanted to see and learn about those lifestyles while they could. José Librado Gurulé (Chapter 11) simply arrived home.

Walk in their shoes. See the scenes they saw. Hear the squeak of the wagon wheels, the braying of the mules, the crack of the whip, the cry of a baby. Wonder at the beauty of the sunrise over a recently drenched prairie. Laugh by the fireside at the end of a long, weary day. Feel what it is like to live in unwashed clothes and with an unbathed body. Know the heartache of loss. Know the thrill of an unknown future. Our youths on the Santa Fe Trail have given us these opportunities.

All these brave and resourceful young people—who told their stories with such honesty and with the power of words that can, even now, take us to their times— left us an immeasurable gift of history and insight. They shared a time that we can only reach out to touch by the words they wrote. And we can use them as models of the strengths we would like to see in ourselves. We can also see some of the intolerance of the age they lived in and hope that we can contribute to a time more tolerant and inclusive.

Their stories are stories of journey. For each, the Santa Fe Trail led to a unique adventure and influence on their life. Learn from their experiences on the stage of history to enrich your own journey through life.

2

CHRISTOPHER "KIT" CARSON
ON THE TRAIL TO FAME

THE ONE MAN WHO stands out for his accomplishments over the history of the Santa Fe Trail is Christopher "Kit" Carson. Kit's life personifies the moving frontier of the early half of the nineteenth century. The years that Kit lived on the frontier were the years of exploration, struggle with the Indians for the land, and the beginning movement of large numbers of settlers across the West. His famous story reflects the larger story of exploration, danger, determination, prejudice, skill, and courage.

Early photo of Kit Carson (PD-US)

Where did this man come from? Why was he such an outstanding figure in a world of rugged men who were carving a nation out of a wilderness? It is very difficult to know anything about his private motivations, thoughts, or feelings because he was a man of few words and never promoted himself. In fact, his modesty minimized his decisive actions throughout his life.

Before he had an impact on our history, Kit was just a teenager seeking his fortune in a frontier town. He walked down a main street with log buildings layered in dust and busy with wagons, oxen, and mule teams. Not very large for his age, a bit slope-shouldered, he walked quietly up the street, dodging through the crowd. His stride was confident without a swagger. It was the smooth, calm gait of a young man who knew his way through the forest while stalking a deer. His purpose was determined though somewhat tentative. He probably wore buckskins and a slouch hat, as other teens did.

His sharp eyes took in all his surroundings. His ears perked to the racket of a caravan of traders preparing to travel the Santa Fe Trail to New Mexico. The noise of men shouting, mules braying, wagons creaking and groaning under heavy loads, and traders dealing with merchants—everything fascinated him. He knew the traders were buying all the supplies they would need for several months' travel across the plains and mountains to Santa Fe. For a young boy seeking his fortune, this was an exciting and challenging scene.

That young boy was sixteen-year-old Kit, destined for fame. A runaway from the apprenticeship at which he had only served two years of his seven-year commitment, Kit had made the decision that being a saddle maker was not what he wanted. The only good thing about it was listening to the tales of the mountain men and trappers who came to the shop for supplies. He loved hearing about the challenges of the frontier, about the wild, uncharted, Indian lands, and he was determined to find his future in that land of adventure.

This adventurous young boy was born in a log cabin in Madison County, Kentucky, December 24, 1809. A year later, his father moved the family to Boone's Lick, Missouri, on the Missouri River, where they cut a farm out of the wilderness. This was the true frontier, where there was little security for the families who lived there. Death, disease, and hardship were daily companions. Often several families would cluster together in a small community for safety. Boone's Lick was such an area that contained defended forts and settlements.

Kit was the eleventh child of his father's fifteen children by two wives. In a family that large, it is often easy, especially for younger children, to feel rather lost in the crowd. His place in this rough-and-tumble family probably contributed to his traits of determination, ruggedness, and individualism. He also proved to be reliable at an early age. His family could count on him to finish whatever task he was given. He tended to be shy and quiet, apparently learning to carve out his own place by actions rather than by words. These traits were the foundations of the man he would become.

The area around Boone's Lick was inhabited by several tribes of Indians who often were hostile toward encroachment on their land. Living with this constant threat of attack required the settlers to patrol, to keep watch, and to farm their fields with their rifles at hand. Kit, like the other children, was taught to carry pieces of red cloth to drop as a trail, in case they were kidnapped by Indians.

Kit's sister recalled that Kit, as a little boy, always had a keen sense of hearing, and at night, if any unusual noise was heard, he was the first to pop up with an awareness that something was out of the ordinary. We don't know whether he ever saved his family from danger in those early years. However, years later, his alertness and sixth sense mitigated the damage of an attack by the Klamath Indians on John C. Fremont's sleeping camp. Kit coped with growing up in this country filled with dangers by developing the skills that would protect him and keep him and others alive.

When he was eight years old, his father was killed. Kit had to give up school and take the family rifle to hunt for meat to feed the family. In those early years, young Kit carried a long, heavy rifle that was about as long as he was tall. Creeping through the undergrowth of the forest, approaching a clearing, crawling into range as he stalked a deer, he had to quietly raise the rifle, steady a shot, and calmly pull the trigger. Knowing either the thrill of success or the crushing defeat of missing a meal for the family must have caused him apprehension that later became confidence and satisfaction. His sharp hearing and eyesight, his ability to be patient and move quietly, his determination to track with skill, and his desire to provide for the family all contributed to his success as a hunter and helper to his mother.

But Kit's character also ran deeper than just honing survival skills. He also knew, as a boy, Indian friends. Not all the frontier Indians in Missouri were hostile. Many were friendly and adaptive to the new influences that were changing their world. Kit was perceptive enough to learn that, like other people, Indians were individuals and tribes were distinctive. Many Americans treated any Indian as a hostile, but Kit never fell prey to that injustice. These early lessons stayed with him when he dealt as a man with western tribes.

From the time he was eight until he was fourteen,

the family was driven into poverty by the loss of Kit's father. Giving up school to help support the family led to a life of illiteracy for Kit. His lack of ability to read gave him a lifelong feeling of inadequacy that he never overcame.

When his mother remarried, Kit was not happy living with his stepfather. We can only guess at what the problems were, but it is a common situation for a boy of fourteen to resent a new male presence in the home. Kit's role in the family changed about this time, and he was apprenticed to saddle maker David Workman, learning a skill he found unbearably dull.

The pull for adventure and escape from boredom, plus the problems at home, grew to a turning point for Kit. In August of 1826, at age sixteen, he ran away from his apprenticeship. David Workman, his master, was required to give notice of his truancy. The following notice appeared in the *Missouri Intelligencer* on October 12, 1826:

> Notice is hereby given to all persons that Christopher Carson, a boy about 16 years old, small of his age but thick-set, light hair, ran away from the subscriber, living in Franklin, Howard County, Missouri, to whom he had been bound to learn the saddler's trade, on or about the first of September. He is supposed to have made his way toward the upper part of the state. All persons are notified not to harbor, support or assist said boy under the penalty of the law. One cent reward will be given to any person who will bring back the said boy. David Workman. Franklin, Oct. 6, 1826.*

---

* Edwin L. Sabin, *Kit Carson Days 1809–1868* (2 vols. Lincoln: University of Nebraska Press, 1995), 12.

Many have felt that David Workman's reward of one cent did not indicate a real desire to return Kit to the saddler's workbench.

Kit signed up as a laborer with a large merchant caravan heading west to Santa Fe across the Santa Fe Trail. He turned from a life of stability and sureness to one of adventure and hardship, but one that would exercise every natural instinct that was in him. He did not seem to mind leaving the security of home. He was a young man who knew what he wanted, and it wasn't a settled life as a saddle maker in a Missouri town. Like many, he responded to what he was good at, because it was those skills that gave him satisfaction. Boys of sixteen in that time were considered on the threshold of manhood, and it was not unusual for them to choose their future course.

How he financed or executed his escape we do not know. When he was trying to hire on to the merchant caravan, he was asked by the trail boss what he had to say for himself. In his humble manner, Kit claimed only that he could shoot. That apparently was enough for the trail boss. He must have seen the undercurrent of confidence in this boy. He was hired as a "cavvy boy," the lowest position in the wagon train. He rode herd on the spare mules, oxen, and horses. It was dirty, hard, thankless work, but it was in the open. He loved riding saddles all day rather than making them at a workbench. Kit thrived with the challenges of travel across the plains, and he soaked up everything he could from the experienced men around him. His keen interest in learning the skills of a frontiersman challenged his natural intelligence. He was delighted with life on the trail. He was beginning to change and mature.

Shortly after arriving in Santa Fe, Kit left and went

to Taos, a Mexican village about seventy miles north. He liked the rough-and-ready life of this mountain settlement. It was the hub of the Southwestern fur trade, and he was drawn to the mountain men who made Taos their headquarters when they were not out on the trap lines. He kept a home in Taos for much of the rest of his life.

Kit Carson home, front entrance

The first winter in Taos, Kit stayed with an old trapper and mountaineer named Kincaid (or Kinkead), who was an old friend of his father's. He applied himself to learning the many skills that he would need for the life of a trapper. He studied Spanish and Indian dialects. He learned to sew his own buckskins, to make a bed of cornhusks, and to make pemmican from his first buffalo kill. He was an apt and devoted student. Though his illiteracy would plague him with feelings of inadequacy all his life, he was able to apply himself and thrive on learning what he needed to know to succeed at what he wanted to do. Survival in the mountains in the winter, depending only on yourself and a few others, required toughness but also a mindset that said, *I can provide anything I need for myself.*

Until Kit proved himself to the other men, he would not be included in any trapping expeditions. So with his usual diligence, he made himself available to every opportunity that was presented until he could demonstrate his worth. Starting in 1828, he signed on to work as a teamster traveling to El Paso (then part of Mexico) and on the Santa Fe Trail as a cook for a company of mountain men. No job was too low or difficult. He had learned enough Spanish to work on a merchant caravan headed to Chihuahua, in Mexico. His persistence paid off in the spring of 1829, when he got the opportunity to sign on with a company of forty Taos fur men on his first trapping expedition. They were going into Apache country on the Gila River.

Trapping was an occupation that he would pursue for a dozen years. It was hazardous but lucrative, due to the popularity of beaver hats in the East and in England. Grizzlies, hostile Indians, hypothermia, killing thirst, and starvation were constant dangers. But Kit mastered the nuances of the trade. He learned how to track an Indian pony, how to set and scent traps, how to wade the icy rivers, how to prepare a pack and pelts, and how to cache furs to prevent theft and spoilage. He became expert with a rifle and a skinning knife. He began to understand how to deal with Western Indians—how to detect ambush, when to fight, when to flee, and how to negotiate. All these skills and more would serve him well through years of experiencing every kind of danger that the frontier could offer.

In the summer of 1835, Kit attended the mountain men's rendezvous on the Green River in present-day

Wyoming. This annual gathering for trade was a real blowout for those who had lived away from society. It lasted several weeks and was attended by trappers, mountain men, Indians, traders—and a few women.

The most popular woman that year was an Arapaho maiden named Singing Grass (Waa-nibe). Kit was attracted to Singing Grass, but there was a rival for her attentions, a large bully named Joseph Chouinard (or Shunar). This French Canadian trapper was known to drink heavily and act badly. People tried to avoid him when he was drinking. When Chouinard insulted Singing Grass, Kit shot him in a duel. He rarely said anything about this fight. Soon he offered the father of Singing Grass a "bride price" of three mules and a new gun, the Indian way of asking for her hand in marriage. They were married, probably in the next year. Kit adored Singing Grass, and by all accounts, they were a happy couple. Kit was now ready to take on the responsibilities of a grown man.

Singing Grass followed Kit during the next couple of seasons as he trapped the rivers of what are today Colorado, Utah, Wyoming, Idaho, and Montana. Kit was now a skilled trapper and navigator of the wild mountains. We do not have much information about Kit's personal life during this period. He did once tell a friend that Singing Grass was a good wife who always had a kettle of warm water waiting in their lodge when he had been out wading in icy water, checking his beaver traps. She would soak his cold feet, and no doubt help to avoid frostbite.

Unfortunately, in 1839, after the birth of their second child, Singing Grass died from complications of the delivery. This was a time when women typically did not have medical attention during childbirth, and many died. When Kit did not mourn in the wailing manner of the Indians, he had to explain to them that he was "crying in his heart." This was a painful time for Kit. Now he had the added responsibility of two young daughters to care for.

In the summer of 1840, Kit attended the last mountain man rendezvous on the Green River. The fur trade was a dying business at that time, due to the popularity of the beaver hat being replaced with the newer-style silk hats that gentlemen were wearing. Kit was drawn to Bent's Fort in what is now southeastern Colorado. Charles Bent, his brother William, and Ceran St. Vrain had built the fort as a trading center with the southern Cheyennes, the Arapahos, and trappers for the market in buffalo hides. For many years, this was the only place of white civilization between the Missouri frontier and Santa Fe. Kit was hired as a hunter to supply meat to feed the travelers and employees at the fort. Friends there helped him take care of his and Singing Grass's two little girls.

In 1841, Kit married a Cheyenne woman named Making-Out-Road. She was apparently beautiful but had a bad temperament. The marriage lasted a mere few months. The Indian form of divorce required only that Making-Out-Road throw Kit's belongings out of the tepee. That showed her displeasure with the marriage and ended it. His real love was Singing Grass in those early years.

In 1842, Kit fell in love with Josefa Jaramillo, the beautiful daughter of a leading family in Taos. They were soon engaged and were married in February 1843. Kit bought a home for Josefa in Taos.

About that time, Kit decided his oldest daughter, Adaline, who was four, needed the influence of an education and should grow up among whites. He didn't

Kit Carson kitchen (the window was a doorway to the garden and oven, shown below)

Kit Carson courtyard

*This is where Kit met with Ute chiefs while he
was their agent*

Kit Carson parlor and office

want her to suffer through life, as he had, because of illiteracy. Kit, known for his ability to act swiftly in any crisis situation, was nevertheless self-conscious about his inability to read and write. He saw it as his failing, though he did learn to put a "C. Carson" on documents. So he traveled with Adaline to Missouri by the Santa Fe Trail, to leave her with family, to be raised in a less wild situation.

He was very relieved when his family accepted Adaline, despite her Indian blood. Many people held a strong prejudice against marriages between different races. Some even considered that a child of a white father and an Indian mother was illegitimate and not to be recognized or respected.

He did not take his younger daughter on this trip. He left her in Taos with the Bent family while he was gone. Sadly, there is no record of what her name was, and Kit never saw her again. She was scalded to death when she toddled into a boiling vat of soap tallow. Tragedy had visited Kit again.

With Adaline in Missouri and Josepha in New Mexico, family life remained elusive for Kit. The difficulty of balancing his roaming spirit with the responsibilities of a home proved a challenge time after time, as he left his family to serve others in some manner. It is hard to tell from this distance whether his choices were selfish or unselfish, but he seemed driven by a sense of duty.

When he worked with someone he admired—especially someone more cultured and educated—he was very loyal to them. He had that kind of relationship with John C. Fremont, the famous explorer. In 1842, Fremont was assigned the task of mapping and describing the course of the Oregon Trail to the South Pass in Wyoming. The government wanted the route made more safely passable for settlers making their way to the Oregon Territory. This was part of the government's strategy to extend the borders of the country from the Atlantic to the Pacific shores.

Fremont met Kit on a Missouri steamboat and learned Kit had a knack for keeping travelers on course and out of trouble. After making inquiries to verify Kit's reputation, Fremont hired him as guide for the expedition. Their mapping excursion became a success, and Kit became a lifelong friend to Fremont and a steadfast advocate. Fremont's report to Congress was glowing about the prospects of fertile land in the Oregon Territory. When reprinted in newspapers all over the country, the news set off droves of emigrants along the Oregon Trail, thus accomplishing the goal of the government.

By 1845, Kit's name was well known across the country as a result of the reports by Fremont. In the many newspaper stories and dime novels written about him, he was described almost as a god. He was renowned as a fine hunter, an excellent horseman, a sure shot, and a negotiator with Indians. He could select a good campsite and set it up or dismantle it in minutes. He could doctor a horse and dress and cook meat. He was a gunsmith, a blacksmith, a fisherman, a farrier, a wheelwright, a mountain climber, and a paddler of canoes or rafts. As a tracker, he would prove time and time again that he was unequaled. He knew how to find grass for the stock, fight a grizzly, locate water, and make smoke signals. He was also a quick judge of people and was known to meet the challenges of life with a cool head and decisive action. The list of skills went on and on. He became an almost mythical figure.

This fame always puzzled him. His shy, retiring nature avoided bragging or telling stories about himself.

When he was approached in the streets on various occasions, he was quite shocked when addressed as though he were a friend with this stranger. He was offended and put off by this forward behavior. It made him want to return to nature and the wide-open spaces. He was most comfortable among the men, like himself, who lived by their actions more than their words.

In May 1846, Kit was again guiding an exploration for John C. Fremont. They were camped at night in the southern wilderness of Oregon on Klamath Lake, when Kit awakened, thinking he heard a noise that was out of place. He looked around the camp but did not see anything that seemed amiss, except that Fremont had not posted a watch. He went back to sleep but was awakened again later when he heard a heavy thud. Kit jumped up to check the noise and saw his friend, the Frenchman Basil Lajeunesse, had his head cut in two with an ax.

Kit yelled out a warning of Indian attack. Everyone sprang to action to defend the camp, except for the two Delaware scouts who were also instantly killed. Kit saw an Indian that he thought was the leader sneak into the camp, and he and others shot the Indian. When the leader was killed, the rest of the braves withdrew. After the short skirmish, the explorers kept anxious watch the rest of the night, but the Indians had withdrawn. The Indians who had attacked were Klamath Indians. In a situation like this, where quick, decisive action was required, Kit always reacted almost without thought. His survival instincts had been honed since early childhood on the frontier.

To avenge the three men he had lost, Fremont delayed their planned departure for California the next day. Kit led ten men, and they scouted ahead until they found an Indian village, which they promptly attacked.

They killed at least twenty-one warriors and burned the remaining village. Their vengeance was satisfied, though they killed other Indians as they circumnavigated Klamath Lake.

The fight between the white men and the indigenous people for dominance in the West was bloody and brutal. Kit had a reputation among some people of being a bloodthirsty killer. He was capable of vicious fighting when thrust into a fight. But he was also known as a gentle man with women, children, and weaker people. He had strong views about protecting the underdog. His role in settling the West no doubt created some conundrums in his character. But when his friend was killed, defenseless in his sleep, Kit helped mete out the punishment.

On June 14, 1846, a group of Californios (Spanish-speaking, mostly Catholic people born in northern California), residents of Sonoma, California, near San Francisco, rebelled against Mexican rule and declared the birth of an independent nation in California—the Bear Republic. Riding south from Oregon, Fremont became embroiled in the effort of US forces to take California from Mexico, and he and Kit arrived on June 25 to find a chaotic scene in California.

On September 5, Fremont asked Kit to ride with dispatches to Washington. Kit mounted his mule and headed east with haste, with a small escort. He was glad for this opportunity to ride across the country to see the nation's capital for the first time. He also planned a visit with Josefa as he passed through New Mexico.

On October 6, Kit and his party encountered General Stephen Kearny and three hundred dragoons headed from New Mexico to California. When Kearny realized he had the astounding good fortune to run into one of the best scouts in the country, he enlisted Kit to turn around and guide him to California over the dangerous route through deserts that Kit now knew. Kit was very disappointed, because after an absence of almost two years, he wanted to see Josefa, and he also regretted missing the opportunity to see the East Coast for the first time. But since Kearny was a general and Fremont only a captain, Kit had to follow Kearny's orders and ride west again. The course of his life was often dictated by duty and patriotism.

The march west across the Gila Trail covered some very forbidding terrain. Horribly hot by day and freezing by night, the journey was brutal on men and animals. When they emerged from the Gila into the land of the Pima Indians, it was like arriving at an oasis. The Pimas were friendly and helped to restore the men to good health, feeding them from their farms.

On November 23, a Mexican courier was intercepted, and his dispatches revealed that the U.S. had lost its grip on California. San Diego was the only place the Americans still controlled, and they were pinned down. This was very bad news for Kearny and his reduced force of one hundred men. Kit was concerned for his friends, especially Captain Fremont. He now felt invested in the effort to get to California to help.

When Kearny's Army finally came upon the first Mexican troops at a town called San Pasqual, the general determined that a surprise attack would be the best strategy, given his troops' weakened condition. On December 6, in the early morning hours, the attack commenced. Unfortunately, the plan went awry when the element of surprise was lost.

With superb horsemanship and their own surprise attack, Californio lancers delivered a bloody beating to the Americans. In close combat and wielding only sabers, the US troops were at a disadvantage—the reach of the longer lances tore the dragoons to pieces. It was a horrible day for the Americans, and they had to concentrate into a defensive posture while the Californios withdrew to the surrounding hills.

The next day, as Kearny tried to march away, he was attacked again and took refuge on a hilltop and dug in. There the troops had to nurse their wounded and dying compatriots with little water or medicine. It was a horrendous scene of blood and piled corpses. The Californios withdrew to encircling hilltops. San Diego was still thirty miles away, and a wounded Kearny and his men were too weak to continue. The general knew he would have to get word to Commodore Stockton in San Diego about the battle at San Pasqual and his need for help. Inevitably, Kit was asked to try to move through the lines of the Californios and get word to Stockton.

On the night of December 8, Kit, a naval lieutenant named Edward Beale, and an Indian named Chemuctah made their attempt to sneak through the enemy lines. It was a dark night with thirty miles to cover through cactus-infested desert. They took their boots off so they could move more quietly through the rocks. At one point, as they crawled on their bellies, a Californio rider on patrol almost stepped on them. They were terrified. Kit determined that they should split up and take three different routes, in hopes that at least one of them would get through. To make matters worse, they had lost their boots in the rocks. Once they could get up and walk, they had to travel through cactus-covered desert, which lacerated their feet.

Kit made it to Stockton's camp the next night. His feet were swollen and cut up. He was relieved to find that Beale and Chemuctah had made it through on their shorter courses. Both men were totally spent. Beale spent over a month in sickbay, recovering from his midnight crawl. It is believed that Chemuctah died shortly after this effort. However, nearly two hundred well-armed men were sent to rescue the Americans.

On the afternoon of December 12, Kearny's Army of the West arrived at the Pacific Ocean after marching all the way from Fort Leavenworth in Kansas. They helped save California for the Americans and much of the thanks went to Kit and his cohorts for getting help at a crucial time. Kit gained additional fame for the struggle he made to get help. Once again, this ability to be in the right place, at the right time, and to pull off an amazing feat, led to his celebrity as a skilled hero who could always save the day. He paid no attention to the celebrity that these exploits brought him, remaining shy and avoiding publicity.

In the spring of 1847, Kit was carrying communications from California to Washington, DC, on the transcontinental trip that he had so wanted. Fremont was now governor in California and had dispatched Kit. On the way east, he was able to visit Josefa in Taos for ten days, after a twenty-month separation. It was the first time that Kit could be home after the Taos Rebellion (see Chapter 1).

During the rebellion, both Josefa and her sister Ignacia—Charles Bent's wife—were in the house during the attack and witnessed the murder. Following the suppression of the rebellion, they had to participate in the trial. It was a traumatic time for both the Bent and Carson families. Many Americans had been killed, and the counterattack by Colonel Price's troops killed many Mexicans and Pueblo Indians.

Sometimes brutality entered the homes of settlers, Mexicans, and Indians alike as the frontier was being contested. One minute all could be safe and tucked away for a quiet night, and shortly there could be blood and a mangled body. We can only imagine what it must have been like for all those involved in the Taos Rebellion, including for Kit to have been away from his family in this trying time. He must have felt that, had he been present, maybe Charles wouldn't have been killed and the families could have been spared the trauma.

We know that people who have witnessed much violence in life can become desensitized. Did this happen to Kit? Certainly not when his beloved wife was involved. But we do know that, as he matured, he seemed to have a growing sense of the futility of the fight between the whites and the Indians, though the Taos battle was not strictly a white/Indian fight.

Kit continued on to St. Louis, where he took a side trip to see his daughter, Adaline, whom he hadn't seen in five years. He must have seemed as a stranger bearing gifts when this child saw him after so long. It is hard to imagine him being warm or communicative with her, though there is evidence that he loved children. It is too bad we don't know more about him as a father. We do know that he made every effort to provide for Adaline's safety, comfort, and opportunities, and he remained determined that she would get the education he never had.

After St. Louis, Kit was able to travel by steamboat and train to the nation's capital. He continued to be taken aback by people crowding to see him. It made him long for the open spaces and the freedom that gave him comfort. Here was a man who lived where most people would only see danger, but he felt more danger when he was among his own kind in a populous situation.

The years had formed a man who wanted the comfort of his family and the people of the Southwest that he had adopted and fought to protect. His comfort zone had changed.

Near the end of May 1847, Jessie Benton Fremont met Kit at the train in Washington, DC. It was arranged for her to act as hostess for him. As Governor Fremont's wife, this vivacious, bright, well-known lady was able to make Kit comfortable in her home. She showed him around Washington and introduced him to all the important people. Kit was a frequent, but never comfortable, dinner guest in the homes of all the people who wanted to be seen with this American hero.

After a few days, Kit was anxious to return to Josefa in New Mexico, but he got an invitation from President Polk to visit the White House. The president couldn't see him until June 14, which was several weeks away. Kit was not happy about the delay, but he couldn't say no to the president. During this extended stay, Kit came to hate Washington, and he didn't trust most of the politicians. The Washington world and its intrigues didn't fit a man judged by actions.

On June 14, Jessie accompanied Kit to the White House. With President Polk they discussed Kit's exploits and battles in the West. The president's plan to make the United States a continental country, sea to sea, had come to fruition with the military successes in California, but President Polk seemed to have little to say about that. After the meeting, Kit left Washington within a few days.

In 1849, when he was thirty-nine, Kit decided it was time to settle down. He wanted to have a home and be with Josefa, despite his wandering nature. Since the start of the Mexican War, he had covered close to sixteen thousand miles on mule back. He started a farm on Rayado Creek in New Mexico Territory, where from sunup to sundown he cleared land, plowed, planted, did lambing and shearing, cut hay to sell to the army, whipsawed pine logs, made adobe bricks, butchered animals, tanned hides, and shod the mules. The work was endless. He and Josefa had been married six years, but he had only been home a few months of that time. The following spring, their first child, a son named Charles, after Charles Bent, was born.

In late October 1849, a group of Pueblo Indians reported that they had seen a white woman in a Jicarilla Apache camp. A company of dragoons was immediately sent to try to rescue Ann White, her daughter, and her servant. They were the survivors of an Indian attack on a small group led by Ann's husband, who had separated from their wagon train to speed ahead by carriage to Santa Fe. When the troops rode through Kit's Rayado ranch, they persuaded him to accompany them. The trail was cold, and he was known to be the best tracker in the country, though in his autobiography Kit mentions working with other experienced trackers Antoine Leroux and Robert Fisher. Once again, duty called him away from his own life and he agreed to serve.

They traveled to the sight of the massacre, forty miles east. The tracks were several weeks old and had been obscured by snow. There was little for Kit to find or follow. The Jicarillas had further complicated tracking by splitting into small groups and meeting each night at a designated location. The search was painstaking work until one day they encountered the remains of an encampment and found a piece of women's clothing. Several days later, it happened again, and Kit became convinced that Ann White was trying to leave a trail, which they followed for twelve days, almost to the border of Texas.

When scouts spotted crows circling, a sure sign of scavenging, Kit discovered a large camp of Jicarillas at rest. Kit immediately began to charge, but Captain Grier and his guide, Leroux, held the dragoons back. Captain Grier thought it would be good to try to pow-wow with the Indians to get back the captives. Kit was furious and thought that was a grave error. He was proved right when the Indians discovered the troops and took off. However, it was too late for Ann White. They found her shot through the heart with an arrow. Kit always felt that, had they attacked immediately, they could have saved her. However, he found her in such horrible condition that he felt she was better off dead.

Kit had become very famous by this time, and authors were turning out dime novels about him. But when he found a dime novel among the possessions of Ann White that told a story of Kit saving a damsel in distress, it had a lasting effect on him. He wondered if she had dreamed of him arriving in time to save her. It was a lifelong regret that he wasn't able to fulfill that dream. Finding that book was poignant and ironic. It always haunted him.

In the spring and summer of 1855, the Jicarilla Apaches and the Utes allied against the whites to fight the US Army. After a costly campaign, both sides agreed to a peace treaty in August. However, the hostilities resumed. Major James H. Carleton was ordered to subdue the Jicarillas. He took Kit as a guide on the campaign. The Indians were defeated and scattered, left in a hungry and near-naked condition. Kit returned to his home in Taos. After a few days rest, he set out on his own to talk to the Jicarillas. He found them in camp and spent a couple of days listening to their grievances.

In September, he reported to Governor Meriwether that he believed the behavior of the Indians was the result of troubles they had had with the government in Abiquiu in 1854. At that time, the government failed to deliver supplies to the Indians that had been negotiated, in exchange for peace. How could the Indians not hunt and wander in their traditional manner, if food that was promised did not arrive? Kit reported that the Indians were desperate and had nothing to live for but revenge.

As much as Kit had fought Indians, he also understood their plight and had compassion for them. Though government policies vacillated, Kit was an early believer that the Indians had to be provided with a homeland where they could practice their own ways and be protected from invasion by white men. He feared they would be exterminated. It says a lot about how the Indians saw him that he could ride, alone and as a friend, into their camp immediately after they had been battling the whites. Kit was a man who had to bridge the past and the future, even as he helped build the future.

During the Civil War, General Henry Sibley led Confederate troops out of Texas to invade New Mexico. Since the 1830s, when Texas won its independence from Mexico, Texans had claimed that part of New Mexico was their territory. Sibley's plan was to conquer New Mexico and then continue on to Denver. The goal was to take the goldfields of Colorado to enrich the financial coffers of the Confederacy.

First, Sibley wanted the supplies from Fort Craig, south of Albuquerque. If he was victorious against the four thousand Union troops there, nothing would stop him from taking Fort Union, further north, which was a central supply center for the military in the Southwest. Colonel Edward Canby was in charge at Fort Craig, where Kit—now a Colonel—was given command of the First New Mexico Volunteers.

Why Kit joined federal troops is not really known. He was not an abolitionist, having purchased three Navajo servants of his own. The enslavement of captured Indians was an old institution in New Mexico, just as the Indians in turn captured women and children from the settlements for slaves. Of course, he had ridden with John C. Fremont and fought with the troops in blue against the Indians and Californios. But most likely Kit's pro-Union stance came from patriotism and loyalty to a greater cause—building a United States, sea to sea.

Kit trained eight companies of volunteers for battle. Colonel Canby had a low regard for these volunteers, but Kit's skills in leadership helped them win respect. Kit had a knack for motivating his men, winning their approval by working as hard as they did.

At the Battle of Valverde, near Fort Craig, Kit's men stood their ground in their section of the battlefield and were winning. When Colonel Canby ultimately withdrew to Fort Craig, what looked like a defeat was really more of a standoff, and General Sibley couldn't obtain the supplies he needed from Fort Craig. His invasion of New Mexico was jeopardized. Even though Sibley did succeed in taking Albuquerque and Santa Fe, Union troops burned his supplies at Glorietta Pass, and Sibley was finally defeated. New Mexico was saved from becoming part of the Confederacy, and Kit and his volunteers had played an important part, since key supplies at Fort Craig were denied to Sibley.

During the years of the Civil War, the Navajos recognized that the Union Army was focusing its strength elsewhere, though they did not understand why. Their raiding to steal and kill New Mexicans along the Rio Grande corridor grew to be a major problem as they took advantage of this lack of military presence.

General Canby was replaced in 1862 by General James Carleton, an experienced Indian fighter. Carleton believed that the Navajos were the reason for New Mexico's backwardness and poverty. How could local peasants ever thrive when they were constantly under the threat of their livestock being stolen and their families murdered? People could not travel and many felt despair and fear.

Through the five years when Carleton served in New Mexico, his old friendship with Kit deepened. This was another time in Kit's life when he seemed to attach himself to a man of better education and become a loyal member of his supporters. Both men saw their task as enforcing peace and security.

Carleton understood that the Navajos could never be beaten in their own land, with their skills at disappearing into their canyon hideaways. He felt the only way to defeat them was to use their own guerrilla tactics and to use a "scorched earth" strategy, like that used by General Sherman to subdue the South in the Civil War. The army would have to go into the Navajo homeland and destroy their ability to survive by devastating their homes, crops, and livestock. Carleton sold his plan to his superiors, in part by convincing Washington there was gold in Navajo lands.

Carleton chose his friend Kit to lead this heartless campaign. Kit begged off. He was tired and wanted to return to Taos and enjoy some of that home life he longed for. Carleton refused to accept Kit's resignation and argued that the people were depending on him. Once again, duty called and Kit answered.

In early July 1863, the campaign to force twelve thousand people into submission began. The Navajos scattered and hid as usual, so it became a long operation of slow destruction. The army demolished wheat fields, cornfields, and melon patches. They wrecked homes and every means of survival. The "scorched earth" strategy culminated in the destruction of the treasured Navajo orchard of peach trees in Canyon de Chelly. Thousands of trees were hacked down. These were the pride of the Navajos. In time, starving groups of Navajos sought peace. They were defeated.

Carleton sent the Navajo people to a reservation in the Bosque Redondo, east of the Rio Grande. The Navajos walked the entire way; about nine thousand survived. Kit then took the job, for three months, of supervising the reservation, but he was not happy trying to deal on a daily basis with the bureaucracy it entailed. This experiment was a disaster, and eventually the Navajos were allowed to return to a reservation in their homeland, but only after many died of disease and hunger.

In November 1864, Carleton sent Kit on yet another campaign, this time to subdue the Comanches who were attacking, killing, and plundering on the plains of Texas. Kit knew this would be a very difficult campaign against some of the best plains fighters. On encountering a Kiowa village of Comanche allies on the Canadian River, Kit's men attacked and destroyed the village, but the Kiowa warriors enlisted the aid of a larger Comanche village further downriver. Kit's men, outnumbered, took refuge behind the walls of an abandoned fort called Adobe Walls. It wasn't long until a mass of warriors, Comanches and Kiowas, made their appearance.

There were about fourteen hundred warriors facing Kit's small force of four hundred. Thanks to the protection of the adobe walls, Kit's men had few casualties through a long afternoon of fighting. Their mountain howitzers contributed greatly to their survival against great odds, because the Indians tried to stay out of the range of the canons. As happened most of the time, the Indians were out-gunned. Kit realized that he could not hold out against such a large force, so he ordered a withdrawal. During the retreat, however, the Indians charged relentlessly, and Kit wondered if his men would survive. But then the Indians ceased their attack, believing that they had taught the army a lesson.

This was Kit's last military engagement, and he was defeated. But the fact that he saved most of his men was a victory too. The debacle could have been worse than General Custer's battle at the Little Bighorn, where Custer's men were all killed due to his bad judgment. But Kit made his decisions very differently than Custer did. He used caution and good judgment. Saving his men was more important to him than any glory associated with winning a fight.

After the Civil War armistice in1865, Senator James Doolittle went west as chairman of a committee investigating the US Indian policy. The Senator interviewed Kit and got the reticent man to open up and talk about his experiences in the West since 1826. In Doolittle's official report of his findings, he quoted Kit's ideas about the Indian policy being developed by the government.

Kit had come to believe that most of the Indian troubles in those years were caused by the aggression of the whites. He was critical of Colonel John Chivington's massacre of Black Kettle's peace Indians at Sand Creek. He felt it was time to set aside areas, near their homes, where the Indians could live in their own manner. He feared the extinction of the race. Doolittle agreed with Kit's ideas. No one knew the West better than Kit, and he wanted a future that included the Indians.

Ironically, however, Doolittle also recognized that the dirty secret of New Mexico was the enslavement of Navajo and other Indians. In Santa Fe alone, there were five hundred Navajo "servants." The United States had just fought a bloody civil war to abolish slavery, but the institution thrived in the West. The country's new laws of manumission would need to be enforced to end the cruelty of slavery in the West.

In 1866–1867, Eveline M. Alexander wrote a diary that was later published as *Cavalry Wife, The Diary of Eveline M. Alexander, 1866–1867*. She met Carson at Fort Garland in Colorado, in the fall of 1866, while he was briefly in command there. He was very friendly and welcoming to her. One day she rode with him to the camp of Ute Chief Ouray. She was surprised at the response of the Utes when they saw Kit. Instead of their usual sullen appearance, she wrote that their faces lit up with joy at seeing him. He delighted one old woman when he shook her hand. She had traveled with fifty Ute scouts during Kit's entire campaign against the Navajos.

Eveline found Kit congenial and open. He shared much of his knowledge of Indians with her. She related that, unlike many Anglos, he believed the Indians should be treated fairly and honestly. He was particularly close to the Utes, and in 1868 he accompanied a Ute delegation to Washington to assist them in drawing up a treaty with the US government.

By 1868, Kit's health was failing. He had an aneurysm in his chest that was growing worse. He made one more trip east to Washington and even visited doctors in New York and Boston, but they told him he didn't have much time. He wanted to get home to see Josefa again, and he endured the discomfort and pain of the long trip home, miles of it riding in a bumpy wagon.

On April 11 he arrived home at Boggsville, Colorado Territory, where he and Josefa had moved their family to the new settlement. Two days later, Josefa delivered a baby girl that Kit named Josefita. On April 27, Josefa died in Kit's arms, as the result of complications from childbirth. Years later, his son said Kit just seemed to pine away after Josefa's death.

His health grew worse. The hard physical life he had lived was taking its toll. Once again he was denied the peaceful home life he dreamed of with Josefa and their children. There was a great deal of sadness in his life with the loss of loved ones. He had to have a strong emotional constitution to deal with all the deaths since his father died. He lost children, friends, and now a second

Carson's grave in Taos, New Mexico

wife that he loved. This was the tragic aspect of his life. On the afternoon of May 23, 1868, Kit's aneurysm ruptured and he died in the arms of his doctor at nearby Fort Lyon, Colorado Territory. He and Josefa had been married for twenty-five years, and they died less than a month apart.

Kit's life symbolizes the story of Western exploration by white men, their determination to build a different society, the energy it took to start that process, and the courage of a single man. He was a trapper while the beaver held out, a trader with the Indians, a guide and explorer with outstanding talents for survival in the wilderness. He was a scout and an officer in the army. He was a mild-mannered leader who could befriend an Indian, try desperately to save a white woman captured by hostiles, and fight when he believed that was the only way. He also loved his wife, children, and his home, that warm place where he could never seem to spend enough time. He was always driven to roam and to contribute, right up until he died.

When we look back at the life of Kit Carson from a very different time and place, there is debate about the kind of man he was. Was he worthy of being called hero, or was he simply the violent hand of Manifest Destiny, the political philosophy of the time, which held that white men had the right to rule the country from sea to sea?

History, with the advantage of hindsight, often judges people outside the context of their time. Growing up with constant danger and the threat of violent death, Kit learned the skills of survival demanded by the cutting edge of a dynamic frontier. Though he couldn't read, he repeatedly proved his innate intelligence and succeeded in his ventures, so much so that he was considered a national hero.

As a teenager, he viewed the Santa Fe Trail as his road to adventure and a life of courage and accomplishment. He never understood the fame his journey brought to him. He was a humble man who simply lived his convictions. Sometimes those convictions led to answering violence with violence, as he had been taught by the ethics of the frontier. At the same time, he was often described as gentle, quiet, unassuming, protective, and respectful of individuals.

In his later years, he had an intuitive response to the shrinking of the frontier and the need for people to get along. His reactions were tempered by the world he lived in. He was caught up between the time when he went west as an enthused young boy to seek adventure and when he had matured enough and seen enough to realize that compromise among people was required.

Kit Carson was the kind of man our nation has always called on to execute the will of the nation. The Santa Fe Trail was his road to freedom and finding his potential as a man of his time. The trail to fame was also, for Kit, a trail to unwanted scrutiny.

3

JOSIAH GREGG

ON THE TRAIL TO KNOWLEDGE

J OSIAH GREGG SEEMED TO start out in life as a scholar. He was born on July 19, 1806, in Tennessee, the youngest son of seven children. In 1812, his family moved to Missouri, where he displayed an aptitude for learning, especially mathematics and sur-
veying. He read widely, be-
coming a schoolteacher at age eighteen. When his family moved again to Independence, Missouri, in 1825, Josiah went with them and studied both medicine and law.

Despite his strong in-
telligence, Josiah's health was poor, and it pre-
vented him from continu-
ing his studies. His condi-
tion began to decline with dyspepsia (indigestion, often

Josiah Gregg (PD-US)

painful) and related complications, eventually degenerating to a point where he could not work or even leave his rooms for a period of a year. In 1830, he was diagnosed with consumption (the disease we know today as tuberculosis).

Unable to provide any effective treatment for Josiah's ailments, his desperate doctors recommended that he travel the prairies, believing that the drier air of the Southwest had been beneficial to some consumption patients. Josiah accepted their suggestion and immediately set about arranging passage with a trading caravan leaving from Independence. Only twelve miles from the Indian border, with access to the Missouri River, Independence had become the thriving hub for outfitting wagon trains and was the embarkation point for westward travel.

Josiah embarked on the Santa Fe Trail for the first time on May 15, 1831. He had supplied himself with the usual flour, bacon, coffee, salt, and sugar. Some beans and crackers were considered extra luxuries for those who could bring them along. In his writings about this experience, Josiah explained that alongside traders and tourists gathered at Independence were invalids seeking cures for many chronic diseases. Liver complaints and dyspepsia were especially considered curable by the diet and exercise provided by travel on the prairie. Josiah learned firsthand the benefits of this cure. He started the trip riding in a buggy, but by the end of a week, he was riding his pony and ready to share the diet of the hunters and teamsters. (A Western horse was often referred to as a *pony*, because it was smaller than most eastern horses.) By the time the caravan reached buffalo country, Josiah was able to take to the chase with his strongest companions, and he found buffalo meat

Two bulls work out their extra energy

the finest of delicacies. He was thriving already on what the prairie had to offer.

This bright young man, who had the courage and curiosity to venture into this foreign environment despite his illnesses, soon found himself loving the travel and adjusting to life on the Santa Fe Trail. This new world offered him challenges that he welcomed. He began to change into a man of the prairie.

In his lifetime, he made eight passages across the trail, spending much of the balance of his time living in northern New Mexico. He kept a journal, which reflects the considerable knowledge he accumulated about the Indians, the Mexicans, and everything to do with life on the prairie and in New Mexico. This journal later became his book, *Commerce of the Prairies*, known today as a definitive text on the Santa Fe Trail. In his stories, we see the blending of his vibrant mental abilities with an innate love of travel and the natural world—something he might not have pursued if the doctors hadn't urged him to go to the Southwest.

In *Commerce of the Prairies*, Josiah wrote about the history of the Santa Fe Trail before 1822. In 1821, Mexico had overthrown Spanish rule and opened their northern borders to commerce with the United States. William Alexander Becknell's first trading trip to Santa Fe in 1821 had proven very profitable. The following year Becknell took the first wagons from Missouri to Santa Fe. Thus, Josiah marked 1822 as the beginning of the trail being a viable trade route. However, it wasn't until 1824, when traders in wagons established a regular seasonal flow of traffic, that the Santa Fe Trail became a true profitable commercial trade route.

Josiah related that the earlier wagons on the trail were the well-known heavy wagons built in Pittsburgh that were pulled by eight horses. When mules became more available, draft horses were replaced by them, because mules held up better under the harsh conditions of prairie travel. After 1829, as many oxen as mules were also used on the trail, especially by big freighting firms. Traders whose profits depended on how much they could haul and the durability of their animals were adapting to the realities of the Santa Fe Trail.

Josiah was a man of detail. He provided many specifics of travel that were of interest to him and which bring the trip to life for us in a manner unique from others who kept journals on the trail. First, he described how the caravan members joined and organized for the long trip. The larger the group the better, in terms of security, but it was often difficult to govern the independent traders.

His writing about his first trip in 1831 is an example of the depth of detail he would include, with fascinating precision. On the second day of travel, the caravan members got a foretaste of what it would be like to travel in inclement weather. They experienced the discomfort of a drizzling rain all day. Josiah described the Osnaburg sheets used to cover the wagons in a manner to protect the cargo and keep it dry in all kinds of conditions. Interestingly, he added the tidbit that placing a Mackinaw blanket between the sheets not only helped protect the cargo but offered a way to avoid customs in Santa Fe and to turn the blanket into a valuable item of trade. Already he was displaying the mindset of a future trader.

The detail he provided makes it easy now for us to picture what the wagon train was like. In the morning the caravan captain called, "Catch up! Catch up!" to signal it was time to hitch the teams. An uproarious bustle followed, with the yelling of drivers to control their animals, the bawling of the resistant livestock, the rattle of yokes and harness. Drivers raced to be first to holler "All's set." When all were prepared, the captain yelled, "Stretch out!" Then whips cracked, dust rose from tramping feet, wheels squeaked, wagons rumbled. "Fall in" was heard, and the wagons spread in long lines across the prairie. Sometimes you can almost smell the leather and livestock or hear the groan of the wagon wheels as the wagons struggled over difficult terrain. Wagon trains were noisy enterprises, even at night. Children yelled and played, mules brayed, parties called from wagon to wagon, coyotes and wolves sang their chilling songs.

During the first two hundred miles from the frontier, no guard was posted over the livestock at night, because there was little chance of plundering Indians. That, Josiah told us, was exactly when they needed a sentry, because the animals were not attached to the caravan yet. In time, the cattle would become as attached to the wagon train as if it was their barnyard, but early in the trip they wandered off, especially during the rainstorms, when they sought shelter. A lot of livestock was lost that way.

There were other incidents involving unsettled oxen. On the first leg of the journey, the teamsters often turned the oxen out at night to graze, leaving them yoked in pairs. This made the morning hitching up easier, as the oxen were still somewhat unruly. However, shortly after dark one night, something set off the herd into a stampede with the rattle of yokes and the thunder of hooves. Fortunately, the wagons were circled in a manner to contain them, or a lot of time would have been lost the next day recovering their stock. Josiah said that oxen can be "whimsical creatures" when in unfamiliar surroundings.

It usually took a while on the trail for the livestock to settle into their routine. All caravans along the trail dealt with such issues. Josiah related a story he heard about a group of traders in 1824, who lost over twenty head of livestock when a stampede of buffalo came near, and their animals ran off with the herd. And he told a cautionary tale about the hunter who got excited and jumped off his horse to shoot buffalo—a rider had to be very careful not to lose his ride. Losing your horse on the prairie could be a quick death sentence.

On May 26, they reached the "joining-up" point at Council Grove, in what is now Kansas, where several caravans would unite for security. Josiah warns us not to envision Council Grove as a thriving village. He points out that upon leaving Independence, they passed the last human abode. From Independence to the borders of New Mexico, not even an Indian settlement would greet their eyes.

The wagon train was re-organized and officers were elected, as their company now consisted of nearly two hundred wagons and various smaller vehicles. They actually had two small cannons for discouraging Indian attacks. At roll call, they had nearly two hundred men, not counting the invalids and other disabled bodies. Every able-bodied man had to stand his share of the dreaded guard duty at night, an often frightening assignment. He related that even the amateur tourist and listless loafer had to do their share of this duty.

Men from every class and sphere of society made up the company. Only a small number of women ventured across the trail. Josiah found it extraordinary that women made the trip, but one Spanish family in their train included females. This family had been banned from Mexico in 1829 by the Mexican Congress but was now able to return home, as the ban had been suspended.

Dress among the caravan members varied according to profession. The city-bred merchant wore the most fashionable coat, with many pockets for carrying a variety of necessities. The backwoodsman wore either a linsey or leather hunting shirt, the farmer his blue jean coat, the wagoner a flannel vest, and others wore a variety of other costumes. They also carried a great assortment of fire arms and knives, creating a party with an outlaw-like appearance.

Daily living conditions were primitive. Kitchen and table ware included a skillet, a frying pan, a sheet-iron camp kettle, a coffee pot, a tin cup, and a butcher's knife. The pan or kettle holding the meal was placed on the grass, and everyone dug in with their dirty hands. Coffee was a mainstay with every meal, even in the hot time of the day. It would be rare to not refill their large cups for a second coffee at each meal.

Josiah's tales of the learning process for those inexperienced caravans illustrated the newness of this phase of westward exploration. There was much learning through error, and Josiah also told funny stories on his fellow greenhorns and on himself. He related how, upon crossing the Cow Creek into known hostile territory, one camp raised many nervous alarms of danger. The first alarm came when a couple of people were chased to the wagons by a group of buffalo, followed two days later by two hunters charging into the camp, saying a hundred of the same "enemy" were at hand. The excitement over that had barely quieted down when another rider arrived on a panting horse yelling, "Indians, Indians!" A screaming bedlam ensued until everyone was armed. Then the howl of a wolf across the creek was mistaken for a human distress call, and everyone went running to save someone in distress across the water. At that point, the camp was left unprotected and open to any enemy, as the men rushed to assist the imagined victim.

Josiah paints a picture of chaos on many occasions when the greenhorns panicked easily at the slightest provocation. After more alarms at Ash Creek and at Pawnee Fork, over signs of the recent passage of Indians, the company began marching the wagons in four parallel lines so that they could form up quickly into a closed circle for defense. The constant alarms helped to keep everyone on a heightened level of observation and alert.

When the caravan reached a place called Walnut Creek, Josiah wrote about a story that happened in the summer of 1826 at this location. A man named Mr. Broadus had reached into his wagon to pull out his rifle, intending to shoot a wolf. He grabbed his weapon hastily by the muzzle, and it discharged into his arm, shattering the bone. Mr. Broadus was advised to have the arm amputated immediately. It was hot in the month of August, and the wound would soon have gangrene. Broadus refused to let them amputate his arm, and gangrene inevitably developed. For several days the other men simply felt they would bury him soon. Though it appeared too late to save his life, Broadus finally agreed to have the arm removed. They had a handsaw, a butcher knife, and a large iron bolt they heated for cauterizing the wound. The arm was opened around the bone, which was promptly sawed off, and the hot bolt was used to close the arteries. Amazingly, Broadus survived and healed in a few weeks.

Though Josiah did not know it, that event was attended by Kit Carson. It had occurred on his initial trip west on the trail in 1826. Kit had witnessed the operation and did whatever he could to help. This episode gave young Kit and Josiah an early idea of the kinds of crude methods that men in the wilderness often had to undertake.

When Josiah's caravan reached a point where they had determined to strike off from the Arkansas River to intercept the Cimarron River, a distance of fifty waterless miles, there was no track or trail to follow. The Cimarron Route was not well established in 1831. They knew it would be a difficult passage from stories of disaster and near disaster that others had brought back when they had explored this route. Every container was filled with water in the hope of not running out. "Fill up the water kegs" was a command no one ignored. The cooks baked bread and prepared food for the two-day journey ahead. Since the prairie was as level as a calm sea, with no landmarks or paths to follow, the compass was their only guide. On the morning of June 14, they departed across the dry country, but on the second day, a heavy rain provided an abundance of water. The worry about water was relieved for a time, but death would visit later wagon trains, due to this lack of water.

Josiah seems to have been able to disengage and observe on his maiden voyage in a manner that really gives us a unique perspective on the learning process that was taking place on the trail. He also possessed an ability to see what was amusing, even in the midst of true dangers. On the day when they encountered a band of about eighty Sioux warriors, the usual alarm went up, and the unprepared traders created a hubbub, scrambling for ammunition, trying to prepare their guns, and bolstering their courage. As the band of horsemen approached close enough to see that they were displaying a US flag, all fear was allayed. Bands that were peaceful would display some sort of flag, if they had one. They held a powwow with the Indians by communicating with the universal sign language of the plains. These Sioux warned of a large group of Comanche and Blackfoot Indians camped ahead.

When the train encountered the hostile Indians, there were many threatening moves and gestures on both sides. The traders marched forth to fight, to the music of fife and drum, but the Indians were more amused than frightened by this strange parade. For all the traders knew, the hostiles interpreted their approach in this novel manner as totally unthreatening. A wise chief offered to smoke the peace pipe, and the crisis subsided. When Indian women and children came poring over a hill, the traders understood — they were outnumbered by nearly a thousand warriors, but the Indians didn't fight when they were on the move with the whole village.

On another occasion, the wagon train was attacked during their noon break. The animals were turned out to graze while cooks prepared dinner. This horde of Indians, believed to be Comanches, appeared about a mile away and charged at full gallop and full cry. When the amateur "cannonries" finally organized to shoot their six-pounder, the Indians had moved off to a safe distance. The first shot fell far short, and subsequent shots caused no damage.

Josiah gives us a nuanced perspective on Indian attacks. He believed that in the course of twenty years of trade on the trail, there had not been more than a dozen deaths on the Santa Fe Trail. However, in 1831 the Indians still were not feeling very threatened by white men moving through their territory. That would change by mid-century, when the escalating flow of traders and settlers changed their attitudes. Hostilities increased as these early trading expeditions grew in number and frequency, further aggravated by whites—who often did not respect the Indians—settling the lands that Indians claimed as their own.

On the last day of June 1831, Josiah's caravan reached Upper Spring, a northern tributary to the Cimarron River. Finally, they could slake their thirst and use water without restrictions. Though they were still a couple of hundred miles from Santa Fe, runners were anxious to leave the slow-moving wagon train and hurry ahead to the city. Generally traveling by night, to avoid hostile encounters, their purpose was to procure warehouses for the goods to be traded, refresh provisions for the wagon train, and to come to agreeable arrangements with the officers of the Mexican customs houses.

The caravan proceeded toward Santa Fe more slowly than the runners, and incidents still occurred. At a campground named Round Mound, the cattle were brought into the circle formed by the wagons parking wheel to wheel. The wheels were then bound with chains and ropes. In the night, as the men peacefully slumbered in their blankets, a dog frightened an ox, and a general panic and stampede spread through the herd. The oxen, despite being yoked in twos, escaped the circled wagons. The next morning, enough oxen were found to hitch the wagons and continue. By the time they stopped for "nooning" at Rock Creek, the train was joined by those who had pursued the runaways. All but a half-dozen of the oxen were found and returned.

The advantage to having oxen when there was such an escape, as opposed to mules, was that the Indians didn't have any interest in stealing oxen. Here Josiah provided us with a detail of this early travel that most history books miss. His personal account informs us of some of the daily trivia of oxen travel.

Fifty miles from Santa Fe, the train arrived at San Miguel, the first settlement of any note. Here the Santa Fe Trail turned south to pass through a gap in the mountains, and then it turned northwest again toward Santa Fe. Josiah reported that the road in this section presented few difficult passages. The route between San Miguel and Santa Fe was, no doubt, well established.

Nearing the city, Josiah began to sense they were arriving in the "suburbs, because of the cultivated fields of corn." Josiah thought he was also looking at brick kilns scattered in every direction. When he commented to a friend on this scene, his friend informed him that those heaps of unburned bricks were houses. This was the city of Santa Fe at last. It was not the expected sight of an exotic and rich capital, but a poor, built-of-mud, small town. This sight was often very disappointing to first-time arrivals.

Though Josiah did not ride ahead with the runners, he did join a group of about a dozen men who rode out to arrive in Santa Fe five or six days ahead of the wagons. He reported that when the caravan began to arrive, it created a great deal of excitement, not only in the community but also among the traders and teamsters. Alert to the close proximity of the city, the drivers had spruced up with washed faces, combed hair, and put on their best clothes. The distinguishing tool of their trade was the long bullwhip with which they controlled the ox teams. There was a great deal of fancy whip cracking and swaggering as the men anticipated the eyes of the pretty senoritas. As soon as their wagons were unloaded at the customs houses, the men had time for some recreation. After their ten arduous weeks of travel, they took full advantage of food and drink, fandangos (dances) held for the arriving caravans, and the many locations for gambling in the relaxed city.

Josiah related that the arrival of the caravan changed the aspect of the city from stagnation and idleness to the bustle and activity of a busy market town. Negotiations among traders, government officials, and local merchants were conducted in Spanish, as the locals did not speak English. The vendors sold their goods to resident shopkeepers or later ran their own emporiums or general stores.

At the end of his story about travel on the Santa Fe Trail, Josiah shared the knowledge of the region that he gained from spending nine years in the area. He talked about the history and the geology of New Mexico, the lifestyles and character of the Mexican people and the Indians, the mines and minerals, the botany and agriculture, the livestock and wild animals, the status and education of women, as well as religion, marriage, and many other topics. He was a keen observer of all that he was exposed to, and he left us with an all-encompassing history based on his firsthand experience.

Josiah traveled the Santa Fe Trail several times between 1831 and 1840, along the way learning to speak Spanish, working as a bookkeeper for Jesse Sutton, a merchant, and by the spring of 1834, he was back on the trail as wagon master of a trading caravan and Sutton's business partner—he was a full participant in the Santa Fe trade. Josiah brought the first printing press to New Mexico that year, selling it to Ramon Abreu, who took it to Taos. He started the first newspaper in New Mexico and called it *El Crepusculo de la Libertad* (*The Dawn of Liberty*).

In the last chapter of *Commerce of the Prairies*, Josiah filled in more details about his time spent in New Mexico. In 1838, he prepared to leave the territory, thinking his move would be permanent. On April 4, his party left Santa Fe with twenty-three Americans and twelve Mexicans. They had seven wagons, one carriage, two small field artillery weapons, along with an assortment of small arms. The major traders in the group were carrying about $150,000 in money and bullion from the last year's trade.

About 130 miles out of Santa Fe, one of the traders, a Mr. Langham, suddenly and unexpectedly died. He was a valued member of the party, but there were no accommodations for a decent burial. He was wrapped in a blanket, and his friends found an elevated spot and buried him before sunrise. He had no tombstone or mourners, other than the company of the wagon train. This was a repetitive theme along the trail. And even though Josiah had commented on the lack of deaths on the trail during his first trip, here he was confronted with one. Everyone who wrote about the loneliness of such burials was very touched by the poignancy of their own mortality.

On April 19, they were camped in the Cimarron valley. All were quietly settled in for a good rest. At midnight, they were awakened by an Indian yell, closely followed by a barrage of gunfire. Josiah characterized the response in the camp as the usual confusion. He described how some awakened from their slumbers and banged their heads into the wagons; some called for their guns, when they had them in their hands; others were clear headed enough that they quickly secured the horses and mules inside the wagon circle from their staked positions around the camp. With the stock secured, the Pawnees lost interest, since their aim was to frighten off, then steal the animals. All remained quiet for the rest of the night. In the morning they found that no men had been injured and no stock lost.

On this trip, there was no threat of getting lost, as the trail was now well marked by wagon ruts the whole distance from the Cimarron Route to the Arkansas River. This well-defined route now relieved travelers of the uncertainties that were experienced earlier in this inhospitable region, as water sources were also now well known. They forded the Arkansas River and journeyed the rest of the way to Missouri without any major disturbances. However, it was fortunate they were carrying a good supply of meat, because after crossing the Arkansas, they saw no buffalo. Josiah commented that he had never before seen them so scarce in this region. Josiah arrived back in Independence on May 11, after a thirty-eight day trip.

In 1845–46, he studied medicine in Louisville, Kentucky. In 1846, he joined General John Wool's Arkansas Volunteers as an interpreter and unofficial news correspondent in the Mexican-American War. After the war, Josiah planned to go into the trading business with Samuel Magoffin, Susan Magoffin's husband (see Chapter 6). However, plans were changed and he ended up back in Saltillo, Mexico, where he practiced medicine for a while.

In 1849, Josiah joined the California Gold Rush. On November 5, 1949, he set out with a group of ill-prepared miners on a cross-country trip in California to find Trinity Bay. The Indians said it was an eight-day trip to the coast, so Josiah's party provisioned for ten days. About six weeks after they started, they emerged on the coast, having existed on deer and smoked game. Eventually, their party split. Josiah's group tried to travel the coast to San Francisco, but snows made the journey difficult. Starvation weakened Josiah, and on February 25, 1850, he fell from his horse and died within a few hours. There is some debate about where he died. His papers, instruments, and specimens were all lost. He had continued seeking knowledge until his final breath.

Josiah was a man with an inquiring mind who traveled widely. He studied and learned wherever he went. It is a loss for us that all he recorded on this last trip vanished. However, he left us a broad scope of information about his earlier travels on the Santa Fe Trail and into Santa Fe. We are in his debt for providing us with such a detailed history of our forefathers and what life was like for them. He certainly provided a unique view of travel on the trail.

From a sick young man traveling west to seek better health, Josiah matured into a seasoned, successful trader. The trail changed his life from one of hopeless struggle with illness to a life of strength, where he could pursue his many interests. Reading his stories, one senses that he was always enthusiastic about the next adventure, always eager to experience and learn more.

He was a man who spent his life exploring and learning. The Santa Fe Trail was a route to knowledge and fulfillment for Josiah.

4

RICHENS LACY WOOTTON
ON THE TRAIL TO SELF-RELIANCE

Rᴵᴄʜᴇɴꜱ Lᴀᴄʏ Wᴏᴏᴛᴛᴏɴ ᴡᴀꜱ a very different representative of the men who settled the West. As a young
man, he set out to make his fortune based on his own
hard work. He seemed to feel a lot of pride in what he
accomplished by surviv-
ing numerous danger-
ous situations and by al-
ways landing safely. He
does not seem to have
the kind of motivations
that Kit Carson devel-
oped in terms of serving.
And he was not the intel-
lectual person that Josiah
Gregg became. He was
a hard-hitting man who
believed in taking, based
on one's strength, with-
out apologies. Much like

Uncle Dick Wootton
(PD-US)

Kit, he mastered many skills. His adventures certainly give us a broad view of what a man could accomplish on the frontier as a result of his own efforts.

Known as "Uncle Dick" Wootton in his later years, his story does not come to us by his own hand but rather through his telling it, as an old man, to author Howard Conard. Mr. Conard spent a summer hearing Uncle Dick relate his experiences to a group of interested listeners. The book was published under the title *Uncle Dick Wootton*.

Though one often senses that the words of the story are not the exact words of this uneducated frontiersman, the authenticity of the story comes out in the details. The author admits to knocking some of the rough corners off the "old timer's" form of expression, but he says the substance of the narrative is true.

Uncle Dick was a good storyteller, with a very sharp memory of the many adventures of his life. Only a few of the men who lived through those escapades with him survived to a ripe old age. Uncle Dick always thought that he had been awfully lucky. He lived for fifty years on the frontier. His many exploits included fighting Indians and befriending Indians, trapping, hunting, guiding, farming, ranching, freighting, driving a stage, and building a life and fortune for his family.

Uncle Dick was born May 6, 1816, in Virginia, and when he was seven his family moved to Kentucky. We don't know about his early years as a boy. In 1836, at nineteen years of age, Uncle Dick made a trip to Independence, Missouri. Commerce between the border town and Santa Fe (then part of Mexico) was getting well developed across the Indian Territory.

Wagon trains of goods had replaced the pack mules

that made the early trips to Santa Fe. When Uncle Dick arrived in Independence, it was the "jumping-off" point for these caravans. Uncle Dick was able to get a position with a wagon train, run by Ceran St. Vrain, that was ready to leave for Bent's Fort, the only settlement between Missouri and Santa Fe at the time (see Chapter 1). Uncle Dick related that, in 1836, he had been away from home long enough to know how to "take care of himself." He could handle a gun and a team, and he wasn't afraid of hard work. For these reasons he got on well as a "wagon man." We begin to see the pride he had in self-reliance.

It took five or six pairs of mules to pull one of the laden wagons across the plains. Several caravans would combine, for safety reasons, as they crossed the wild country. The train Uncle Dick was a part of had fifty-seven wagons with 150 men. That size was not at all unusual.

Tall tales abounded in the west and Uncle Dick may have made up some stories or exaggerated others. One story that has been attributed to both Uncle Dick and Kit Carson probably never happened. But Uncle Dick claimed the story as his own. He related that when they had gotten about a third of the way down the trail without any mishaps, Uncle Dick was standing guard one night. He had been warned to shoot at anything that moved beyond the area where the mules were staked out to graze. When he saw movement and watched it for a while, he decided that the movement was a hostile and that an attack was imminent. His shot awakened the camp, but on investigation, it was found that he had shot Old Jack, one of the lead mules. It was hard to live down that mistake. According to Uncle Dick, Old Jack had disobeyed orders, gotten loose, and strayed beyond the perimeter! This was typical of his ever-present humor.

By the time the train reached Bent's Fort, Uncle Dick had made his reputation as a frontiersman. He had been in his first skirmish with Comanches, shot his first buffalo, and succeeded in driving a wagon across the plains—all by age twenty. Young men could make their mark pretty quickly where there was a shortage of laborers.

Uncle Dick was soon chosen to lead a group of thirteen men on a trading mission with the Sioux Indians. It seems he had to be a young man with much confidence to undertake such an assignment so early in his experience of the West. He led the men north with ten wagons of beads, trinkets, knives, ammunition, blankets, and some old guns, to find the Sioux. When they found Indians, they would camp near their village until it was determined if the Indians wanted to trade. Then they would send a rider and mule with goods into the village and set up commerce in a friendly lodge. The whites traded for Indian furs, buckskins, robes, and ponies. In exchange for a good knife, for example, they could get a buffalo robe. They wintered in 1836–37 near Fort Laramie (probably called Fort William at that time) in what is now Wyoming.

Another of Uncle Dick's stories that has not been corroborated may have been a corruption of a real event or just a tall tale. He told of how later, after returning to Bent's Fort, he was with a group of eight men who rode out to meet a wagon train and offer an escort along that portion of the trail known to be vulnerable to Indian attack. A year before at the same location, troops of United States soldiers had been attacked by Comanches and were badly beaten. On that occasion, the American horses were not accustomed to frontier fighting and were stampeded by the whooping, charging Indians, making it easy to pick off the troopers one at a time. As Uncle Dick's party rode out, they were very aware of that history and were on high alert. They succeeded in bringing the caravan safely to the fort.

Uncle Dick told of the time when he rode out with a group, and the Pawnees attacked. In their effort to stay out of rifle range, the Indians didn't do damage to Uncle Dick's party. However, Uncle Dick's party killed thirteen of the sixteen Indians. These frontiersmen were well armed and were very good shots. The other three Indians surrendered at the wagon train and were taken as prisoners. Uncle Dick and the others extended the same courtesy to these detainees as the Indians extended to their captives: enemies held in an Indian camp were shown hospitality. They might immediately be killed once released, but they were not killed in camp. The Indians would also sometimes let one man in a battle live to return and tell his comrades what had happened. Uncle Dick and the others fed their captives and turned them loose to carry home the story of their defeat. This is not always consistent with many stories of captives that we have, like Ann White's story in Kit Carson's experience. Uncle Dick had an interesting variation to offer.

One year Uncle Dick earned $4,000 in profit from nine months of trapping. He felt that a couple of years more like that, and he could go home, rich enough to retire. However, as time went on he found himself tied to the mountain life, and though on one other occasion he planned a trip east, he never returned home. After his parents died, he felt those old ties were broken. He was now committed to a new life.

In 1838, Uncle Dick set out on the longest trapping trip ever made by Americans. His group of nineteen men trapped the Arkansas River to its source in Colorado, then followed the rivers of northern Colorado, the Green River in Utah into Wyoming, the Big Horn River into Montana as far as the Yellowstone River, the Snake and the Salmon Rivers in Idaho, the Columbia River in Washington, and ultimately sold many of their pelts in Vancouver, Canada. They traveled south through Washington, Oregon, and California to San Luis Obispo. They followed the Colorado River to the Gila River, all the while trapping. When they finally got home, they didn't know how long they had been gone, as they had lost both their almanac and the sticks on which they were marking time. Uncle Dick's group of nineteen men had been gone for nearly two years. Only fourteen returned. The others were lost to Indians. It was considered a successful trip.

In 1840, Uncle Dick was returning to Bent's Fort from Taos when he ran across an Arapaho woman who had escaped the Ute Indians. The Utes had defeated the Arapahos in a recent battle. He provided her with food and safety for a day or so, and then she returned to her village. When she told her tribe members of how Uncle Dick had cared for her and saved her, they were very grateful. Never after that did Uncle Dick have any trouble with the Arapahos, even when they were on the warpath. They taught everyone in the tribe about this good white man and were Uncle Dick's friends ever after, thus demonstrating a sense of honor that few whites acknowledged when dealing with Indians.

As the economy of the West changed, men like Uncle Dick adapted and applied their skills to new trades. When trapping became less profitable, Uncle

Dick contracted to hunt for Bent's Fort, as Kit Carson had done. His job was to provide them with the large amounts of meat they needed for residents and travelers. He said there was no more exciting and better sport than hunting buffalo. Herds would darken the ground as far as a man could see. He didn't think he was far wrong when he said there had been millions of buffalos on the prairie. (Some current-day estimates go as high as fifty million.) Uncle Dick couldn't imagine, in those years, that there would come a time when all the buffalo would be gone.

One day in the fall of 1840, after having shot twenty buffalo, he was waiting for the butchers, who regularly followed the hunters, to arrive and start their work. He noticed a pair of twin calves and decided it would be fun to raise them. He mixed the calves with his milk cows, which adopted them into the herd naturally. He eventually sold them to a zoo in New York, but for a while he was a buffalo rancher. Here was a man who was willing to try anything.

Another occupation that Uncle Dick undertook was courier between the forts owned by Charles Bent and Ceran St. Vrain. In 1842, they ran a weekly express from Bent's Fort to Fort St. Vrain, north of what is now Denver. Uncle Dick claimed to have carried as much as sixty thousand dollars' worth of silver on pack animals without ever losing a dollar. He seemed proud of that accomplishment, a testament to his honesty. However, it is probably an exaggeration again because there was not that much silver involved in the fur trade in 1842.

In the winter of 1843, Uncle Dick turned his many frontier skills to Indian trading because of the profits that could be made. He obtained a license to trade with the Ute Indians who lived sometimes in the Mexican territory and sometimes across the line into the United States territory. In the US territory, the license prohibited trading alcohol to the Indians, so Uncle Dick abided by that rule on both sides of the border. He had a stock of vermilion and other paints, beads, knives, ammunition, and guns. Though the Utes were peaceful at the time, he had to avoid running into the Apaches, who were hostile.

He and his Delaware Indian helper had a bad scare when they set up camp near a village they thought was inhabited by Utes. As they entered, however, they realized they were among Apaches. Fortunately, the braves were out on a hunt. Uncle Dick and his helper lost no time in mounting their horses and putting as much distance between that village and their camp as they could, knowing that if the warriors had been home, it surely would have been the end of them. Once again, he had spectacular good luck.

When they finally joined the Ute camp, they found out that an important chief lay dying. They knew this was bad news for them, because a Ute custom was to kill the first stranger in their village after a chief died. They really needed to conclude their trading while the chief was alive, and they tried to entice the Utes to commence trading, but it was a nerve-wracking three days before the Indians became interested. They traded their goods as quickly as they could and departed. They found out later that the chief died two days after they left the village.

Uncle Dick described some of the customs of the many tribes he knew. He said the wives of the Comanches were miserable drudges. He thought the courtship practices of the Shoshones were unique. He related that the girls were more fleet-footed than the braves. When a suitor made known his preference for a maiden, he had to run after her and throw a rope over her, indicating they were tied for life. If the young woman didn't favor the suitor, she would outrun him, but if she was amenable to the match, she let the suitor catch her. Uncle Dick had a wealth of such stories about the tribes, as he knew so many of them from firsthand experience.

In some tribes, if an Indian couple wanted to divorce, they were free to separate and marry again. If there were children, they became the responsibility of the grandparents. Uncle Dick humorously speculated this was a system that would be popular with the crowned heads of Europe and, maybe, some people in the U.S. However, things were different among the Comanches, where a divorced woman had her ears and nose cut off, and she became an outcast—a much harsher system.

Along with marriage and divorce practices, Uncle Dick knew a lot about the various religious beliefs of the different tribes. He also told of how the Indians loved to gamble. On one occasion, the Utes went to Trinidad (Colorado) to have horse races against some whites who were not experienced in the ways of the Indians. Uncle Dick observed that the Indians ran their slower horses for a while to get the measure of the whites' horses. Then they challenged the best-blooded horse that had been brought from Kansas City with their fastest horse, and they won. Their jockey was a little boy that they tied to the horse for the race.

On one trading trip with the Utes, Uncle Dick had a Shawnee Indian with him. One day the Shawnee saw a Ute that he recognized had shot one of his tribesmen, and he killed the Ute. Uncle Dick knew they were in big trouble, because the Ute camp was nearby and there were only about eight men in his group. Uncle Dick led them in a hasty retreat, but a large party of vengeful Utes soon picked up their trail. They were caught in the open where they could not use terrain to their advantage. The packhorses were circled and used as a fort, within which Uncle Dick's men prepared to fight. Because they had much better guns, they were able to kill some of the Utes and a lot of their horses. In time, the Utes gave up the fight and left them to their hasty retreat from the area.

Uncle Dick had so many close scrapes like this that he began to wonder at his luck. He felt he had a charmed life. He realized his good fortune probably gave him the confidence to undertake adventurous actions that others avoided. He became convinced that, whatever the future held for him, he would not be killed by Indians.

While Uncle Dick related many hair-raising stories about encounters with Indians, he also talked about many other dangers to those who were trying to get a foothold in that country in the 1840s, things that people later in the century didn't have to encounter, due to diminished populations of wildlife. He talked about wild animals, especially wolves. But one of his encounters was with bears, which typically avoided human contact. He was hunting in the Cimarron Mountains, only about a hundred yards from camp, when he struck a grizzly trail. He followed it a short distance and stepped into a clearing where the bear was located. Unfortunately, the bear was in the company of four other fully grown grizzlies. He admitted he was looking for a bear, but he hadn't intended to run into a whole convention!

He knew that to shoot one or two of the bears would lead to the others attacking him and shredding him with their claws and teeth. He knew that to retreat would likely incite a bear charge, so he decided to stand his ground but not behave in any aggressive manner. The bears eyed him for a short time and then started growling at him in a very threatening manner. After about five minutes, the bears decided he wasn't hostile, and they ran off in various directions. He felt he had been very lucky and that their behavior had been more forgiving to his intrusion than he had any right to expect.

One of the bears was so anxious to get away that he ran directly into and through their camp, scattering sparks from the fire where some of the men were roasting venison. Uncle Dick related that bears knew the sound of the snapping of the cap or clicking of the hammer of a gun before firing. They knew what the sound meant and it enraged them. That was just part of the reason that he didn't fire that day.

At the time of the Taos Rebellion in 1847 (see Chapter 1), Uncle Dick was at his farm in Pueblo, in what is now southeastern Colorado, when the people in that area got word of the rebellion and the murder of Governor Bent. It was their inclination to march to Taos to avenge their many friends who were killed, but they had no idea of what was going on there. They didn't know if the rebels had been reinforced by Mexican troops. After much discussion, the men decided that, though there were probably enough American troops in Santa Fe to take care of the matter, they should help out. Private citizens often volunteered to back up military troops.

Five men started for Taos, and it took several days to make the 165-mile trek. When they arrived in the mountains above Taos and looked down on the town, they saw that no troops had arrived, so they waited. When Colonel Price arrived from Santa Fe, they made their way down the mountain at night to join the camp of the troops.

The soldiers and the rebels fought all the next day, and Uncle Dick thought the battle was as hard fought as any of the Mexican War. Eventually, thirty-five volunteers, including Uncle Dick, got to the wall of the church where the rebels were gathered, knocked a hole in the wall, and threw shells into the church, killing many there. The troops hunted down those who escaped from the church, and the rebellion was ended.

Shortly afterward, Uncle Dick enlisted as a guide with Colonel Doniphan's force of about eight hundred men. They were ordered to march to Chihuahua in Mexico to join forces with General Wool. Uncle Dick's responsibility was to scout ahead for enemy forces, select the best route of travel, and find suitable camping grounds that had sufficient water for so many men. This was not an easy task in dry Chihuahua. Food was scarce, so some of the troops decided to lasso wild cattle to butcher. They soon found that the cattle were capturing them, as they were dragged around by their ropes!

When they were eighteen miles short of Chihuahua, Doniphan asked Uncle Dick to make a return trip to Santa Fe with dispatches. Uncle Dick wanted to see the famous city of Chihuahua but agreed to make the trip. He traveled by night, made no campfires, slept little and ate less as he traveled alone through enemy territory, avoiding detection. In about two weeks, he delivered his dispatches with a great deal of relief. After that, he made Taos his home for several years, where he had a business.

In 1851, Uncle Dick decided to make a trip to St. Louis, where he had not been since 1835. He wanted to buy stock for his merchandising business. On a bet, he rode through in the record time of a little over seven days. For his return trip west, he had to wait for some time to ship his goods, due to low water levels in the Missouri River. When he got to the jumping-off point at Westport, he had to pick up his horses and unload his goods from the steamboat for loading on wagons. He discovered that cholera had broken out in the area. He said that he wasn't afraid in the mountains or fighting Indians, but when it came to cholera he was a coward. He didn't want to be "carried off" by an epidemic "the first time I crossed the borderline of civilization." So he got his horses, arranged for his shipping, and put 150 miles between himself and Westport in forty hours. He knew there wouldn't be any cholera in the Rocky Mountains.

In 1852, always open to a new way to make a fortune, Uncle Dick realized that the thousands of people flocking to California as a result of the Gold Rush were encountering a scarcity of food supplies. In New Mexico, a sheep cost one-tenth of what it could bring in California. There were large flocks in New Mexico, and he bought about nine thousand head of sheep. He knew that driving sheep over sixteen hundred miles had never been done—especially over mountains and barren plains and deserts. They had problems with some Ute Indians, but Uncle Dick's long experience with them got him through that menacing scrape.

When they reached Salt Lake City, Uncle Dick rode into town to resupply. He met Ben Holladay, an old freighter and stage owner who had operated the Pony Express. He also met Brigham Young, the founder of the city and leader of the Latter Day Saint movement, who invited him to dinner at his house. Uncle Dick hesitated to go because his clothes were in such bad shape after many days on the trail, but he went and enjoyed the visit, especially the wine that the "head of the church" served. Two days later, he left Salt Lake.

Uncle Dick had misgivings about some of the men he was able to hire to help him on the drive. Eventually his instincts were proven correct. One day, he decided to ride ahead of the herd, to lie down and get some rest. He told the men to awaken him when they got that far, but when he woke up, he could tell from the tracks that the herd had passed him. He believed they thought the Indians would find him and kill him. He soon discovered that a half-dozen of the malcontents were leaving small groups of sheep along the road for a wagon train that was following them. Their intent was to pay their passage with the caravan to California. That night, he single-handedly confronted and disarmed the men and sent them away. He assumed they joined the wagon train, and he had no more problems with his help.

Uncle Dick camped twelve miles from Sacramento, California. The trip had taken 107 days, and they got through with 8,900 of the 9,000 sheep they had at the start. Uncle Dick spent the rest of the winter in the Sacramento area, disposing of his sheep. On his return trip, Uncle Dick passed through the country of the peaceful Pima and Maricopa Indians. As with other travelers, Uncle Dick was impressed with these tribes. They were handsome, friendly, industrious, generous farmers. He arrived home on January 8, 1853, just under eleven months from when he had left.

Uncle Dick told of having carried as much as $14,000 in gold—and more in drafts—from California. He commented on how safe it was to travel with a lot of money then or to keep money in one's home. He attributed this security to the quick justice of the times. Several of his stories related how a criminal could be captured, tried, and hung all in one day. He felt this swift "justice" added a remarkable protection to property. He defended the right of citizens to take the law into their own hands if authorities couldn't or wouldn't assure that criminals would receive punishment. He was a man little dependent on any authority other than himself.

While Uncle Dick lived on the Arkansas River, farming and ranching, he was always able to have good relations with the Cheyennes and Arapahos of the area. When they came to his place, he would trade with them, and their visits were friendly, even when they were on the warpath. Much like Kit Carson, he was able to work out a peaceful co-existence with some of the Indians. He felt that the authorities could not protect him from Indian depredations, so he had to do it himself. He did that by trading with the Indians, even when not licensed by the government. He kept that business between himself and the Indians.

Uncle Dick had learned how to survive and thrive in the wilderness, despite the hardship and danger. He felt sympathy for the settlers who followed the early mountain men across the Santa Fe Trail; many didn't fare so well. In the summer of 1855, he knew of a family that left Independence, Missouri, to resettle, consisting of a young man of about thirty, his wife, two small children, and the wife's mother, a woman of about fifty. When this family arrived in Indian country, both of the children got sick and died. Then, two weeks before they arrived at Uncle Dick's place at Pueblo, Comanches attacked them, and the young man was fatally wounded and died. When the wagon train arrived at Uncle Dick's, the young woman hadn't recovered from the shock, and she soon died. The grief-stricken older woman was so pitiful that even the men were shedding tears. There was no way for the woman to return to her friends back east, so the people of the wagon train took her with them, promising to care for her the best they could. Uncle Dick knew of this kind of tragedy being repeated many times with the privations that the emigrants encountered. He felt compassion for them and no doubt believed their fights against the Indians were justified.

When Uncle Dick was relating his stories of settling the West, the wagon trains and stagecoaches had been gone from the prairie for ten years. But he still dreamed of what it was like to handle the reins of six or eight horses or to "whack" a team of oxen when he did freight hauling for the government. In 1856, he recalled, he had taken a wagon train from Fort Union, in northeastern New Mexico, to Kansas City, Missouri. He left us a vivid and detailed description of a wagon train. He described the "prairie schooners," teams of five pairs of oxen, herds of spare animals driven along, the number of men it took to move such a train, how they organized, and the profits to be made. In the 1850s, Uncle Dick did a lot of freighting for the government, hauling supplies for the forts and the troops that manned them. It was a profitable but arduous business, yet one that he loved.

Uncle Dick also left us with many particulars about how the early stage lines worked. It was a very rough way to travel before there were any passenger way stations. Travelers were responsible for their own defense when attacked by Indians, so they liked to have as many armed men as possible among their eleven passengers. The trip between Independence, Missouri, and Santa Fe, New Mexico, took about two weeks unless there were interruptions, like Indian fights or broken equipment. It cost about $250, and each passenger could have forty pounds of baggage. Hard tack, buffalo meat, and pork made up the menus. They traveled day and night for the whole trip, so any sleep was gotten while sitting up. Passengers could get out and walk when they tired of the jostling of the stage.

In October 1858, Uncle Dick again thought of going east. He had decided to take his profits and return to the States as a comfortably retired man. He set out with several wagons of goods to have one more trade with the Indians and to wrap up some affairs in the Rocky Mountain region. When he arrived in the area that is now Denver, his plans and his life were changed. There were a few hundred gold miners in the area. Men who wanted to buy his trade goods, because there were terrible shortages in the area, soon bombarded Uncle Dick. Even though the profits would have been better trading with the Indians, he was soon convinced to stay in Denver until he sold all his goods. He again decided to give up the idea of going east and planned to spend the rest of his life in the mountains, recommitting his life to the West. He replenished his stocks and set up a business. Eventually he built a hotel, but he didn't do well, because he was constantly feeding starving miners who had no money.

There were times when the prejudices of the time were personified in Uncle Dick, as might be expected. He never understood the concept that Indians had a right to protect their land from invaders. His point of view was always in line with the philosophy of Manifest Destiny, a general notion prevalent at the time in the United States. According to Manifest Destiny, it was the duty of Americans to remake the West in the image of agrarian America. It was considered the right of white Americans to take from the "savages" the land between the Mississippi River and the Pacific Coast for purposes of "civilization."

For example, Uncle Dick felt it was justified when, on November 29, 1864, Colonel John Chivington led eight hundred troops against peaceful Southern Cheyennes at Sand Creek. Chief Black Kettle was abiding by army restrictions on where his village could camp for the winter, and the tribe was living peacefully, not participating in raids. Yet Chivington and his men killed between 150 and 200 Indians, mostly women and children. To Chivington, there was no distinction between Black Kettle's people and the hostile tribes who were responsible for raids.

Unlike Kit Carson, who distinguished friendly Indians from hostile ones, Uncle Dick saw them all as troublesome. They were "all right" as long as they were friendly and made no objection to white men taking their land. And Uncle Dick felt that "tender-hearted Eastern people" were just "Indian lovers"—a term he used pejoratively.

One of Uncle Dick's primary claims to fame was the building of a toll road through Raton Pass. He knew that Raton Pass was a natural highway through the mountains between settlements in southeastern Colorado and northeastern New Mexico. Both freight companies and stage companies wanted a route south from Trinidad, Colorado, toward Santa Fe. A trail through the pass existed, but it was only passable by saddle horses and pack animals. Wagons and stagecoaches could not make it through, especially in the winter.

Uncle Dick obtained the appropriate charters from both Colorado and New Mexico Territories, and in the spring of 1866, he started the vast project of building a road through the mountains. There were hillsides to cut, rocks to blast, and bridges to build. When the road was completed, it was a good road that gave Uncle

Dick pride. However, he found that some people in the West did not understand the idea of a toll road as Easterners did.

With stage companies, freighters, and the military, he had no problem collecting tolls because they needed and wanted the road. Uncle Dick did not charge Indians for passage, because he knew they had no concept of tolls and he didn't want trouble with them. They usually came up to the gate and asked permission to pass, which they were given. Sometimes they offered some compensation for the privilege. However, many New Mexicans did not want to pay a toll. They were pleased with the road and liked traveling on it, but they looked upon the toll as an obstruction that no man had a right to impose on a free-born native of the mountains. Sometimes Uncle Dick used diplomacy to settle the disagreement and sometimes he used a club, but he always got payment.

The last fight with the Utes in his area was in 1867. In 1878, when the railroad took the place of the stage lines, Uncle Dick's life totally changed. With the removal of the Indians, the disappearance of game, the end of the stage lines, and the transfer of freight hauling to rail cars, his era of "stirring adventure" was over. Uncle

Seeing New Mexico from the top of Raton Pass

Dick was ready to enjoy the prerogatives of old age, but he missed the wildlife, the Indians, and the stage line running through his area. When he heard about some of the other old timers from his mountain days having passed away, he felt nostalgia for the days of danger and challenge they had shared.

Uncle Dick died in 1893, having outlived five wives and seventeen of his twenty children. It was the same year that the United States Census Bureau declared an end to the American Frontier. The frontier had been a line defining populated areas and wilderness areas. The whole country was now considered populated.

What can we conclude from the generous sharing of Uncle Dick's stories? He was adventurous enough, as a very young man, to head into the unknown to seek his fortune, and he was successful enough to survive and thrive. He became a rugged, tough man. He had to learn the many skills of a mountain man, and he certainly worked at a great variety of occupations, adapting to his changing times. He also could tell colorful, often times exaggerated, stories about the exploits of his life.

But he also had many of the prejudices of his time, especially toward the value of the Indian and vigilante justice. Those are hard traits for us to admire. Like Carson and Gregg, Wootton was a man who performed according to the expectations of his time. Though we might not always agree with his philosophy, we can understand that he was the kind of young person who contributed to the changing of the West.

Uncle Dick never mentioned his personal feelings about anything other than his adventures, where he took pride in his honesty and the fact that he made his way by being totally self-reliant. The reason why Uncle Dick does not mention his family or his personal feelings can only be guessed at. Was it because he thought the adventures and dangers of his life were all that would interest others? Was it a macho belief that men didn't deal with feelings? Was it because he only evaluated his own life in terms of his ability to win and survive? Perhaps talking about so many family members who pre-deceased him was too painful for words. We will never know the answers to these questions.

Similarly, little is known in any firsthand way what Kit Carson's feelings were, but we learn about the kind of man he was from others' recollections. Gregg wrote with sophistication about the many facets of life he had observed in New Mexico and beyond, but he also spoke little about his emotions. It is wonderful that we have a record of the accomplishments of these three men and of all that they can tell us about life on the trail, but we don't seem to have an opportunity to know them very well in terms of their inner selves. Nevertheless, we can conclude that a man known as "Uncle Dick" was able to relate to people in a manner that earned their respect and affections. His determination to rely on no one but himself, as expressed in his ability to learn any job, is proof of the success of his quest on the trail to self-reliance.

5

FRANCIS PARKMAN JR.
ON THE TRAIL TO DISCOVERY

FRANCIS PARKMAN JR. WAS born into a wealthy Boston family on September 16, 1823. Though he completed a law degree at Harvard Law School, his true goal was to be a historian and writer.

He grew up in the same manner as most boys of the time from privileged families. He had several opportunities as a young man, but he chose not to follow his father into the Unitarian clergy or to follow others that he knew into the practice of law. His paternal grandfather, a rich merchant in Boston, left enough of a fortune for Francis to follow a literary vocation without any monetary worries, though health issues would

Francis Parkman
(PD-US)

perpetually plague him, and he fought against incapacity from eye problems and arthritis throughout his adult life.

Francis entered Harvard College in 1840. In 1843, he had a breakdown that forced him to take a seven-month leave and to travel in Europe. He returned to college and completed Harvard Law School in 1846. When he had a recurrence of an eye problem, he had the excuse to take more time to travel—this time on the Santa Fe Trail. He drove himself to develop endurance by making trips to the mountains of New Hampshire and Maine. The "year of decision" is what Francis called 1846. It was the year that he went west and when the war with Mexico began. Many emigrants were bound for new homes along the frontier, and many soldiers were in transit to or from the war.

Francis decided to travel west on the Oregon Trail and returned east by the Santa Fe Trail, writing in his journal about what he observed and experienced, including his feelings about all that he saw. He recognized that America's westward expansion spelled doom for the Indian tribes and the buffalo herds, and he wanted

to study the native cultures before they disappeared. He longed to experience the buffalo hunt, Indian warfare, and the village life of Indians. He was determined to study the manners and character of the American Indians and their culture before it was altered or obliterated by the influence of the white people. Despite his debilitating illnesses, he persevered in his historical research and writing, sometimes using helpers as his eyes but always refusing to idealize Indians. Francis left us a true and poignant picture of their worlds. What a gift!

In the spring of 1846, he traveled with his friend and relative, Quincy A. Shaw, to St. Louis, Missouri, on a journey of "curiosity and amusement" to the Rocky Mountains. They were among the privileged who were now tourists on the trail. Francis related that St. Louis was a bustling place, with emigrants from all over preparing to travel to Oregon or California, many of whom he described as persons of wealth and standing. An unusual number of traders, engaged in commerce, were preparing their outfits for the journey to Santa Fe, New Mexico. Hotels were crowded. Gunsmiths and saddlers were kept busy. Almost every day, steamboats, crowded with passengers, left St. Louis heading west to the trail's jumping-off point. It was an exciting time and place.

Francis and Quincy departed from St. Louis on the twenty-eighth of April. The steamboat's upper deck was crowded with large wagons loaded for the Santa Fe trade. The travelers brought on board a band of mules and horses, saddles and harness, and other sundry items needed for travel across the prairie. A small, two-wheeled French cart was hidden among the other articles of travel carrying the equipment that Francis and Quincy would need on their long journey. The assortment of passengers included traders, gamblers, speculators, adventurers, emigrants, mountain men, Negroes, and a party of Kanza Indians.

Once Francis's group reached the town of Westport, where they would begin their westward land travel, they ran into Captain C. (Francis's nomenclature) of the British Army. He was traveling with his brother and Mr. R. (also Francis's nomenclature), an English gentleman. They had all previously met in St. Louis. Because this English hunting party was too small to venture over the prairie alone, they proposed joining up with Francis and Quincy. This seemed agreeable. The Englishmen were well outfitted and had a Canadian hunter, Sorel, in their employ, along with an American muleteer, Wright. Additionally, a trapper named Boisverd joined their party. He was seeking numbers for security, just as they were.

When large numbers of emigrants preparing to travel west from nearby Independence, Missouri, heard that there were twenty-three hundred Mormons preparing to travel from St. Joseph, Missouri, this news caused a great stir. Most of the Independence emigrants were from Missouri and Illinois, where they had learned hatred for the Mormons. There was the fear of these two well-armed groups clashing on the prairie. In Independence, the emigrants asked Colonel Stephen W. Kearny (later General Kearny), Commander of the Third Military Department, for an escort, but they were refused. As it turned out, the emigrants from St. Joseph were also Christian and there was no problem. To avoid trouble, the Mormons left later in the year, after most of the other wagon trains had already gone ahead. Religious war is not a new phenomenon.

After seven or eight days, preparations at Westport were complete, and Francis and his party undertook their departure. Immediately an obstacle arose. A shaft mule objected to being harnessed, and reared and plunged until she almost threw Francis and Quincy's cart into the Missouri River. Soon she was traded for a better-trained mule. However, Westport was barely out of sight when the cart got stuck in a muddy gully. It was not an auspicious beginning for these greenhorns. Francis saw the humor in their troubles and managed to maintain the disengaged observer bearing that a writer needed.

Francis mentioned restlessness, love of the wild, and hatred of cities among his motivations for undertaking this trip. However, Quincy was also going in hope of improving his health, so they both were part of the new tourist class as well as health seekers.

As they set out, Francis described their party. He strongly admired their hired guide and hunter, Henry Chatillon, who totally won Francis's respect during the trip. He described Chatillon as having an athletic figure, wearing a blanket-coat, a broad-brimmed hat, moccasins, and pants of deerskin. He carried a knife stuck in his belt, his bullet pouch and powder horn, and his rifle. He seems to have been the epitome of the frontiersman.

Francis's friend Quincy rode a little sorrel and led a spare horse. Their muleteer, Delorier, followed with their cart of provisions: tent, ammunition, blankets, and presents for the Indians. Delorier was a French Canadian. Fatigue, exposure, nor hard work ever seemed to impair his cheerfulness or gayety. This parallels the descriptions of a later traveler, Lewis Garrard (see Chapter 7), with regard to the contributions of the French Canadians on the trails.

Soon they met Indians from the Kanza tribe, on a begging mission to Westport. Francis found them to be very poor and degraded, writing that they represented the ruinous effects of close proximity to whites.

When they encountered a Shawnee village with a Methodist mission, he was impressed with their agriculture. Both in appearance and character, he found the people in marked contrast to the Kanzas. Their chief had a lovely, large farm and a number of slaves, which demonstrated they had adapted to the new culture that was forced onto them. When they next came across a Delaware Indian, Francis again made comparisons. This once proud tribe was now much diminished due to their warlike culture. The Delawares fought against other remote tribes until their numbers were significantly reduced. In contrast to the Shawnees, they had not adapted.

When Francis's party arrived at Fort Leavenworth, in present-day Kansas, Colonel Kearny welcomed them and extended the courtesy to them that he was known to provide. Despite the fort's name, it was without defensive works. It was not threatened by war and was a tranquil post.

To quench Francis's curiosity with regards to the Indians, they visited a Kickapoo village. With each such encounter, Francis described how the Indians dressed and lived. He described the Kickapoos as having faces painted red, green, white, and black, wearing calico shirts, red and blue blankets, brass earrings, and wampum necklaces. They swarmed over the traders' store and had to be watched against stealing. They, in turn, watched Francis's party with suspicious eyes. Their ponies and their village were in a poor state, with houses in ruin due to neglect.

Returning to the fort, they visited with a trader at his establishment and enjoyed the luxuries that he offered.

Iced water, glasses, and excellent claret rounded out the afternoon's pleasures. On return to the fort, Francis called upon Colonel Kearny and then returned to their nearby camp, ready to depart in the morning and resume their journey.

One morning during breakfast, Henry Chatillon suddenly gave a shout of alarm. Everyone looked up and saw their entire herd of twenty-three mules and horses running back to the settlements. After a race of a mile or more, Quincy was able to catch a horse, mount it bareback, and head off the herd. Many had broken their hobbles, which were supposed to prevent their escape, resulting in bad sores on their legs. It wasn't uncommon for livestock to try to return to the settlements, but it was dangerous to lose the animals and be left on foot.

It wasn't long until it became apparent that within the English group there was some dissension. Captain C. came to Francis's camp one day and complained that Mr. R. was making all the decisions without consulting anyone and imposing his ideas on everyone. Francis investigated these charges and found that Mr. R. was a peculiar person who seemed to think he knew everything, and he was riding roughshod over the quiet-mannered captain. Francis related these nuisances of personality quirks in a very humorous manner. He had a dry, subtle wit that analyzed without becoming perturbed. He noted that if Mr. R. said it was going to rain for a while and then the sun would shine, but then the sun came out and it rained later, Mr. R. didn't seem to notice the discrepancy.

Francis's group had been following the St. Joseph's Trail, and on May 23, they arrived at the junction with the Oregon Trail. As they sat around their fire, they heard the distant sound of men and women laughing.

After eight days of not encountering any other humans, it was a wild and impressive sound. Soon the leader of a twenty-wagon emigrant train came into their camp. His wagons were waiting for the rest of their party, which had stopped for a woman who was giving birth. These were the first emigrants they had encountered, though they often saw the sad evidence of others when they passed a gravesite that had been torn up by wolves. Once they saw a sad marker that said, "Mary Ellis, Died May 7, 1845. Aged Two Months." This was a common and sobering occurrence along the trail.

Though Francis's party preferred to travel separate from the emigrant train, getting stuck in the mud ruined their evasion. Before they knew it, Mr. R. invited four of the wagons to join their group. Others were irritated that Mr. R. summarily made such a decision, but Francis felt these new men were strong additions against the danger of Indians. They had reached a point in their journey where they felt there was a good chance that the Pawnees would try to rob them. They set up three watches each night, with two men on each watch to stand guard. When Francis was on watch with Delorier one night, he wondered how steadfast the muleteer would be in the face of an attack. He asked Delorier if he would run if the Pawnees fired on them. Delorier responded with a decisive "Oui, oui" ("Yes, yes" in French). Francis was not surprised at the answer, except in how honest the confession was.

Francis was a well-educated man who expressed, with touching prose, the wonder of some of what he saw. At one point, he described coming over a summit and laying eyes on the Platte River Valley:

> We all drew rein, and, gathering in a knot on
> the crest of the hill, sat joyfully looking down

upon the prospect. . . . [I]t had not one picturesque or beautiful feature; nor had it any of the features of grandeur, other than its vast extent, its solitude and its wildness. . . . [H]ere each man lives by the strength of his arm and the valor of his heart. Here society is reduced to its original elements, the whole fabric of art and conventionality is struck rudely to pieces, and men find themselves suddenly brought back to the wants and resources of their original natures.*

Men of all backgrounds were often struck dumb by the emptiness and wildness of this vast land, knowing it had stood as they saw it for centuries.

In the Platte Valley, Francis and his companions located a small group of bull buffaloes one day and immediately took up the chase. As the bulls split in different directions, Francis was separated from the other hunters as he chased a small group over the extensive hills. His horse, Pontiac, was terrified and hard to control as he ran down one bull, but Pontiac was also unstoppable in the excitement of the chase. When the bull spun around and charged, Pontiac capered out of the way, almost throwing his rider. Francis shot the bull with his pistol, but failed to hit it in a fatal location. This was a dangerous thrill for a young man!

Francis gave up the chase as the bull lumbered away and only then realized he was lost. He had no idea how many miles he had run or in what direction. He had a small compass and determined he should ride north to intercept the Platte River. However, at this point, the course of the Platte swung away from its normal easterly

---

*   Francis Parkman Jr., *The Oregon Trail* (New York: Penguin Books, 1985), 105.

course, and Francis headed in the wrong direction to find it. After two hours he realized he was in real danger of being seriously lost. The prairie offered no landmarks to break up the undulations of rolling, nondescript land. Francis decided that his best guide to the river would be the buffalo. He selected a buffalo path to follow that was at right angles to his course. He was reassured that this was a good decision by the freer gait and perked ears of Pontiac, and sure enough, the path led him back to the river. A cool head was a good thing to have on the prairie—some people did get lost and never were found.

Francis was well educated and sensitive in a way that was different from the people around him. They were mostly tough and uneducated, but basically good, hearty people, seeking a better life. We don't know if they appreciated the scene around them. Surely most did. But Francis recorded for us a wonderful picture of his feelings about his surroundings.

One day, Francis sat down on one of the many buffalo skulls that surrounded their camp. It was a good site that offered water and grass. He noticed the great variety of flowers that flourished in this peaceful spot. As he contemplated their delicacy, their rich colors, their frail textures, he marveled that it was so rare to have a moment in this harsh, rugged environment to notice these details of nature that reminded him of home. A train of thought took him back to New England and the well-remembered faces of loved ones, so far away. He felt the flowers represented the good things that existed in this environment, but he wondered what was here to replace the ennobling influences of his gentler homeland.

One day, when their group encountered a large village of Dakota (Sioux) Indians on the move, Francis described a young warrior who was in the lead. He was nearly six feet tall, lithe, graceful, and strongly proportioned. His skin was clear and delicate and without paint. His long hair was gathered behind and held with talismans of magic. From the back of his head hung a string of glittering brass plates that were very stylish. His chest and arms were bare and his buffalo robe had fallen to around his waist. The decorated moccasins on his feet completed his attire. He was a typical specimen of a Dakota warrior in everyday dress.

Then he described the chaos of the moving mass of people relocating their village. These people appeared noble to him with their tall stature, unique dress, and free society. The chief, Old Smoke, made quite an admirable figure, with his favorite and youngest wife carrying all his weaponry and a group of stately leaders nearby, all clad in white buffalo robes. At the same time, a long train of emigrant wagons crossed the creek. Francis seemed to grasp the significance of the movement of these two races passing each other and the enormity of the clash of cultures. He understood the white culture would decimate these innocent nomads, and he wrote about it with irony and poignancy.

As they approached Fort Laramie in what is now Wyoming, realizing that they were pretty shabby after six weeks of not attending to grooming, Francis's party stopped by the river to shave and try to clean up before re-entering society. Francis felt the exercise was almost futile, since the water they used from the Platte River looked "like a cup of chocolate."

Built for the fur trade with the Indians, Fort Laramie was a post of the American Fur Company. When Francis arrived there, he found Fort Laramie short on hospitality. Once their letter of introduction was read by a literate clerk, they were given a large room that was finished barely better than a barn. There was a bedstead with no mattress, two chairs, a chest of drawers, a tin pail for water, and a board for cutting tobacco. There was a fresh scalp on the wall suspended on a nail. This was the best that the fort had to offer.

It wasn't long before the door of their room was silently pushed open and a tall Indian entered and shook hands. Then he seated himself on the floor. Soon others followed. These were men of standing who expected to smoke a pipe with the new visitors. A pipe was lighted and passed around. This was the only entertainment that their visitors expected.

While at the fort, Old Smoke's village arrived, the emigrant trains arrived, and even Captain C. and Mr. R. arrived. Despite the lonely, empty miles of the wilderness, there were busy locations where many arrivals provided interest, company, and business to be conducted.

Francis was anxious to pursue his purpose for traveling west. Since he was a child, he had been curious about the Indians, but he couldn't find satisfaction for his curiosity by reading. He was glad to find that the summer of 1846 was to be a warlike summer, for the western Dakotas had suffered reverses the summer before at the hands of the Snake Indians, and they were planning revenge. Francis hoped to observe their preparations. They were to be led by the son of a prominent chief, named Whirlwind. Whirlwind had sent messengers out to the tribes to meet at La Bonte's Camp, on the Platte River, to prepare for war.

Francis wanted to observe firsthand the nature of the Indians—their vices and virtues, their modes of life, their government, their superstitions, and their domestic behaviors. He resolved to live among them to accomplish this. He became determined to attend the rendezvous at La Bonte's Camp. However, an Indian called The Horse brought word to the fort that Henry Chatillon's Indian wife was deathly ill in the camp of the Whirlwind. Plans were changed to accommodate Chatillon's desire to visit his wife before she died and to make arrangements for their children. So it was determined to go to the camp of the Whirlwind and join him in the journey to La Bonte's Camp.

Shortly before leaving Fort Laramie, Francis became very ill with stomach cramps and was very weak. He chose to travel anyway, but he was plagued throughout most of the rest of his travels with whatever had gotten into his system. He could barely sit a horse, but his determination prevailed.

When Francis joined Whirlwind's camp, he observed the indecision of the Indians about what their next move would be. The Indians did not have a leader, but each man acted on his own to do what he wanted to do. They were nomadic, and when the village set out to move, some might go one place and some another. Chiefs like King Philip, Pontiac, and Tecumseh had tried at various times to get bands of Indians to act as one, but the results were never very successful. In this case, the Indians could not decide whether to proceed to La Bonte's Camp or not—much to Francis's frustration.

Francis continued to be plagued with dysentery that left him very weak. He found his days passing in camp, in a very languid manner. As he later wrote his book, he had been unaware of how dangerous his situation really was at the time. Weakness in the wilderness was a serious handicap. A man's very survival at any moment might depend on his vigor and stamina.

After some time, Whirlwind and his compatriots decided to move, but not to La Bonte's Camp. They planned to go into the Black Hills to hunt buffalo, desiring to get enough meat for the winter and enough hides to replace their lodge covers. They would also go to a specific area where they could cut lodge poles for their tepees. This created a problem for Francis and Quincy. Should they go to La Bonte's Camp when they didn't even know if other tribes would show up there or should they travel to the Black Hills? In the end, they decided to go with what was sure, and they remained with the Dakotas.

On July 1, both the Indian camp and Francis's broke up and started traveling toward the Black Hills. However, in a short time, a messenger from Fort Laramie arrived saying that a friend of Henry Chatillon's wanted Francis's party to join him at La Bonte's Camp, where the messenger assured them that ten or twelve villages of Indians would assemble. After a council, Francis's group decided to change course, and they separated from the Indians the next morning.

They waited all day for the trapper Bisonette to meet them as planned but finally proceeded toward La Bonte's Camp without him. Upon arrival, not an Indian was there. Francis was very disappointed and only found out weeks later that the lack of buffalo in the area caused the Indians to camp about twenty miles away. At the very time that Francis expected to join them, they were performing their war-preparation ceremonies that he so wanted to observe.

After wasting several days at La Bonte's Camp, Francis decided to try to catch up with Whirlwind's village in the Black Hills. Quincy decided to return to Fort Laramie. The friends agreed to meet at Fort Laramie on the first of August.

Francis selected one of the men to go with him, even though he knew that his health was very bad and it would be dangerous. He was quite determined to pursue his original purpose of living among the Indians of a tribe. The next morning he set out on his trusty little mare Pauline, whom Francis called fleet, hardy, and gentle. She was laden down with his equipment and needs. For food they had a leather bag of flour and a smaller one of tea, along with weapons, powder, a tightly rolled blanket, and a small parcel of Indian gifts. His travels were very difficult due to his sickness and the rugged terrain. His horse also got desperately sick, and she could hardly drag herself along. It was a dire situation because, though heavily armed, Francis did not have the strength to defend himself. In the wilderness, the loss of one's mount was tantamount to death, but Pauline kept struggling forward and eventually recovered.

Raymond, Francis's companion, warned that they should not keep going because they were entering the range of the hostile Snakes, Arapahos, and Gros-Ventre Blackfeet. However, Francis remained determined to complete his purpose, and they continued with Raymond's quiet acquiescence.

Francis was pleased when he was finally able to join the camp of the Ogallala branch of the Sioux tribe. Here was his opportunity to live among the Indians and learn about who they were. He regarded them as savages. This tribe had not had much contact with white people, and their way of living was little altered. Though Whirlwind had changed his mind about going into dangerous country, most of the rest of the tribe had adhered to their plan to hunt buffalo and cut lodge poles.

With the influx of emigrants and the dwindling of the buffalo that the Indians depended on, Francis anticipated great changes coming for the Indians. He foresaw the harmful effects of the presence of the military, availability of whiskey, and the corruption of their culture. He sensed the destruction of their nomadic lifestyle. With the coming of security on the prairie, he also felt the danger and charm of the country would disappear.

Francis provided a marvelous description of everything about the Indians and their village. The sounds, their dress, their social interaction, and their daily actions were brought to life by his pen. He described sitting around a fire in a tepee at night with shadows dancing on the walls, listening to the men tell their tales of war and hunting. As the fire flared up, the lights danced on the warriors' weathered faces, and then as the fire died down again to darkness, Francis felt the uniqueness, danger, fascination, and mystery of the scenes these men depicted. It gave him a sense of an ancient time that was fast disappearing. His skill in writing about it permits us also to experience the passage of time between then and now—it can even raise goose bumps, so vivid are his stories. We can truly feel a kinship with these people of the past.

As the Indians penetrated deeper into the land of the Snake Indians, establishing campsites with defensive features became more important. On one occasion, they camped in a low area that caused unease in the white men and the Indians. Francis noticed a naked warrior high on the tallest bluff, keeping watch, and he was told that scouts had ridden out in all directions watching for the enemy. For many reasons, life could be precarious in that time and place.

When the exhausted hunters arrived back in camp after each day of hunting, the women immediately provided them with food and water. Soon the warriors were asleep on buffalo robes. Now the work for the women began, as they did all the butchering, curing of hides, and drying of meat. For five days they were in this camp and for three days the hunters went out for meat. They hunted buffalo successfully, with enough meat and hides to supply the tribe for the year. But the whole camp was uneasy and on the alert. Young men were constantly scouting the area for signs of danger.

One night, Francis heard an old woman haranguing a dog that she was about to kill with one blow, for stealing a prized piece of fat. She was informing the dog why he did not deserve to live. Francis's observation of the scene provides us with an interesting bit of Indian philosophy. He noted that the Indians believed that inferior animals understood speech and were intelligent. In many cases, they perceived a spiritual affinity between themselves and an animal, even considering that they descended from a deer, wolf, bear, or tortoise. This gives us some insight into what their religion was and the spiritual quality of their commonality with nature.

Francis's host, Kongra-Tonga, afforded insights into the role of father and husband for Francis. Typically, the Indian fathers and mothers loved their children. They indulged them to excess and rarely punished them. On those rare occasions when they did punish, they would throw a bowl of cold water on the child. This *laissez-faire* approach fostered wildness and a sense of liberty, which made them hard to govern as children and as adults. Kongra-Tonga liked to play with his favorite son, a small toddler who tried to dance to his father's chanting song.

Francis found Kongra-Tonga less exemplary as a husband. The older wife that Kongra-Tonga lived with took good care of his lodge and children, but his affections were expressed for a younger maiden in a separate lodge. One day, when she displeased him, he threw her and her belongings out of the lodge. After this divorce, he returned to his main lodge and sat peacefully smoking, in seeming satisfaction.

On the first of August, Francis realized he was late for his rendezvous with Quincy. It was a two-day ride to Fort Laramie. To make his journey swift and safe, Francis offered a handful of bells and a paper of vermilion to Hail-Storm to guide him back to the Fort. Hail Storm was pleased with that offer. The next morning as it grew light, Francis set out from the camp and looked back. He saw that the camp was all a bustle, preparing to be on the move again, to a forested area where lodge poles could be harvested. It was difficult to take final leave of his Indian friends. For a while, the swarm of chiefs, children, warriors, women, maidens, dogs, and horses poured down the mountain as Francis watched. It was a grand and imposing scene that Francis felt his pen was inadequate to describe.

When Francis could finally see Fort Laramie from miles away, he had to sit for a moment. He felt he was looking at the very center of comfort and civilization. It was a relief when he met Henry Chatillon, Quincy, and Delorier. They had begun to worry about Francis.

The time arrived for Francis's journey back east. The first leg would be to travel south from Fort Laramie to Bent's Fort and then pick up the Santa Fe Trail. They had been warned not to travel this route with less than twenty men because of the danger of hostile Arapahos, but many of the companions they had planned to travel with had already departed. So Francis and Quincy were accompanied by only Henry Chatillon, Delorior, and Raymond.

Francis commented that he and Quincy were seasoned wilderness travelers by this time. All they needed was a horse, a rifle, and a knife. Those were all the necessities required for survival and contentment. He wrote that Henry Chatillon had no fear and Delorior and Raymond no thought, so there were no objections to traveling in this small company. On the fourth of August, they bid a final goodbye to the hospitality of Fort Laramie.

During their journey, they met their trader friend, Bisonette, who invited them to stay a few days in his camp with some Sioux and Cheyenne Indians. They met an Indian called The Stabber, who told them the story of encountering six great war parties of whites along the Arkansas River. He hadn't known there were so many white men. He told of them riding large horses, carrying long knives and short rifles, and wearing splendid war dress. That was how Francis's party understood that dragoons and a voluntary army were passing up the Arkansas River. The Stabber also saw many white "lodges" drawn by "long-horned buffalo." These were, no doubt, caravans of military supplies being pulled by oxen. He had also met a Comanche, who told him of Mexicans and Americans fighting—and that the Americans were victorious. This wilderness telegraph was how Francis and Shaw learned that the Americans had entered a war against Mexico.

Once again, Francis provided detailed descriptions of the camp activities that the Indians engaged in. During the day they raced their horses and at night danced war dances, but they blocked Francis from being close to the dances. This was not the place for a white man. However, in the dark, Francis found a spot where he could observe the dances without being noticed.

When they arrived at a location called the Fort at Pueblo, they found a mean and shabby area surrounded by a mud wall. They were shown to what Francis called, tongue in cheek, the "state apartment." This mud room was furnished with a crucifix, a mirror, a picture of the Virgin Mary, and a rusty pistol. A meal was prepared for the guests and served off a blanket on the dirt floor. There were no chairs, but a number of boxes to sit on. Francis said this seemed luxurious to them.

Over their meal, they heard the latest news of the Mexican War. General Kearny had left Bent's Fort three weeks prior, to conquer Santa Fe, and an old newspaper informed them of the battles of Palo Alto and Resaca de la Palma in Mexico.

Since the passage of Kearny's troops, which provided security across the plains, the trail east from Bent's Fort had become very dangerous with hostile Pawnees and Comanches. Many men had been killed, and a large number of horses and mules had been stolen. Regardless of all the warnings not to travel with a small group, they decided to take their chances and leave from Bent's Fort with only Henry Chatillon and Delorior as escort for the six hundred-mile trek back to the frontier of Missouri.

From Pueblo to Bent's Fort was about seventy-five miles, and by noon on the third day of travel, they arrived within three or four miles of the fort and made camp. They hung a looking glass against a tree trunk and made a primitive toilet. Then they rode into the fort.

It looked like a swarm of locusts had invaded. The grass around the fort had been eaten by the horses of General Kearny's Army. Most of the stores of the fort had been picked clean. It was hard to get enough supplies for the planned trip across the prairie, homeward bound. All within the fort was dull and lazy after the bustle of the army's departure a short time before.

At Bent's Fort, Francis and Quincy made the acquaintance of a little man in military attire. His unpronounceable name became Tete Rouge because of his mop of unruly red curls. He appeared to be more suited to mint juleps and oyster suppers than the hardships of the prairie. He was a silly, foolish fellow who lived off the efforts of others. He had joined the army for the adventure of fighting the Mexicans, but on the trail west was taken ill. When General Kearny and his troops left Bent's Fort for Santa Fe, Tete Rouge was left behind with the invalids. After awakening in his sick bed one morning with a dead bedmate, he felt an urgent desire to depart as soon as possible.

On August 27, Francis, Quincy, Chatillon, and Delorier were ready to leave Bent's Fort for the frontier of the United States. Tete Rouge begged so diligently to join the group on their trip back to civilization that finally they agreed. He ultimately provided them with much frustration, entertainment, and, at times, danger. Three men from California also asked to join Francis's party, again for security reasons. Ellis, Gurney, and Munroe were good men to add to their small group.

The big, splendid horses Francis's party had left the States with had long since been traded for the hardier, rough breed of the West. They also now had difficult-to-handle pack mules and badly worn equipment. Tete Rouge immediately displayed his incompetence handling a mule, which he could not catch or saddle. He soon proved so dangerous with a gun that they kept him unarmed. He was always present wherever there was food, though, and grew fat on the trail.

Only a few days out of Bent's Fort, they met a long train of wagons belonging to traders headed to Santa Fe. Francis wrote in his journal that this train belonged to the trader named Magoffin (see Chapter 6), whose brother came across the river to visit and share information.

They knew that hostile Arapahos were in the area. The whites had seen their tents on the horizon, causing a lot of anxiety. They also knew General Kearny had been through the area recently and had warned the Arapahos that if they attacked any white men, he would annihilate them. So Francis hoped the Arapahos would be on their best behavior. He elected a strategy of entering their camp to visit and showing no fear. Francis, Quincy, and Chatillon rode boldly into the Indian camp, while the others hurried on to get as far away as possible before dark.

Francis thought the Arapaho village resembled a Sioux village in every way except cleanliness and neatness. A guide led them to the chief's lodge, where threatening-looking members of the village closely surrounded them. A bowl of meat was offered to them, but no pipe. That was not a friendly sign. They held their horses with them at all times and made a bold exit as soon as they could.

At a safe distance, they made camp for a few days so that Henry Chatillon could hunt enough buffalo to supply Francis's group with meat for the last month of travel. Chatillon was an excellent hunter. Quincy was startled one day when creeping through the grass to stalk buffalo, and he came upon Chatillon, surrounded by these large animals. Quite unaware of being observed, Chatillon stood at his full height, a strong figure, leaning on his rifle and assessing the herd around him. Periodically he would select a fat cow, raise his rifle, shoot her dead, reload, and resume his stance. The buffalo seemed oblivious to him. The bulls rolled in the dust, bellowing and butting each other. Sometimes they would sniff at the dead beast. Once in a while, a bull would face Chatillon in amazement, but they weren't inclined to attack.

When Quincy spoke to Chatillon, he was told to stand up and come forward. While the buffalo gathered around their dead companions, Shaw was able to shoot five bulls before the buffalo decided to decamp. Chatillon knew the behavior of these animals because he had studied them. He took pride in his hunting skills. He seemed to have a spiritual connection with these monstrous beasts.

They spent a few days hanging the supply of meat that Chatillon provided and allowed it to dry for travel. After four days, they had about five hundred pounds of meat for the rest of the trip.

Our intrepid travelers met the Missouri Volunteers under Colonel Price, on their way to Santa Fe to fight in the Mexican War. Francis found the men they talked to were somewhat rough in their manners, but he could not deny their bravery, their intelligence, or their character, which was free of meanness. Their heroic qualities made it easy to overlook their coarseness.

On the fourteenth of September, they met a very large caravan bound for Santa Fe. Since Francis had been suffering again from the disorder he had while traveling with the Sioux, he sought the care of a doctor who attended the wagon train. The doctor prescribed calomel. Francis was so desperate for some relief that he took the "poison" that night instead of eating dinner.

After a long day of travel with no water, they came to a broad valley with a significant stream. Both animals and men found relief from their horrible thirst. In the valley were camped the Mormon Battalion and more of the Missouri Volunteers on their way west. Francis related that the Mormons were to be paid off for their military service in California and allowed to set up new communities, so they had wives and children with them. He found a great contrast between the military discipline of the Missourians compared to the half-military, half-patriarchal religious "fanatics" who planned to establish an empire in California.

Francis was not happy to see so many camped in the valley. His party found solitude a quarter mile from the stream. From that day they met, almost every day, government wagons bearing military supplies for the troops. These trains moved at a snail's pace toward Santa Fe.

When they arrived at the campsite at Cow Creek (according to Josiah Gregg, about 249 miles west of Independence, Missouri), they discovered the novelty of ripe grapes and plums. At the Little Arkansas River, a little further on, the landscape began to change from the arid deserts with short buffalo grass to a richer, greener country with flowers.

There was nothing to be feared now from the local Indians—Sacs and Fox, the Kanzas, and the Osage Indians. Francis appreciated their good fortune in having traveled for five months with a very small force through a dangerous country and not one of their animals had been stolen. Three weeks after they reached the frontier, the Pawnees and Comanches began hostilities along the trail, killing men and stealing horses. They attacked all size parties for the next six months. Francis's luck had held out.

When they reached the trail cutoff that led to Fort Leavenworth, they were glad to be rid of Tete Rouge. He was anxious to collect his military pay for the valuable services he had rendered, Francis commented, sardonically.

At the outskirts of civilization, Francis welcomed the sights and sounds of beauty that included birds and trees, yet he had mixed emotions. He welcomed the end of hard travel, but he felt a longing for the wilderness of prairie and mountains that were behind. Despite the illness he had suffered through the summer, even in later years, as he wrote about the experience, he felt a strong desire to visit those wild places again.

At Westport, they sold their horses and their equipment to others headed west. They hired a wagon and drove to the Kansas landing where they again received hospitality and sat on a porch and looked down on the Missouri River. The passage to St. Louis took eight days. They returned to the Planter's House and retrieved their trunks. Then they traveled for two weeks by railroad and by steamboat to arrive at their familiar homes.

As a footnote to his story, Francis felt he had to pay tribute to their guide, Henry Chatillon, who served them with skill, zeal, and fidelity. Chatillon always showed the greatest respect for his bosses. Francis respected his sincerity, honor, and generosity of spirit. He had a great regard for the feelings of others. He was a true gentleman. He could not write his name and had lived in the coarsest of conditions, but he represented the best of mankind. Chatillon was always humane and merciful. He could be as gentle as a woman and as fearless as a lion. In a world that was often brutish, Chatillon maintained an admirable chivalry.

Francis wrote a fascinating, detailed account of all that he saw on this great adventure, motivated by a need to understand the peoples who owned this land before the white men arrived. There were times when he reflected some of the prejudices of his time, as others traveling the Santa Fe Trail did. However, on the whole, he left us an exciting account of what travel across the Santa Fe and Oregon Trails was like.

He traveled into the land of the Dakota Indians while it remained as it had been since the first encounters of the white men and the Indians. He was enthused by all the opportunities that came his way to observe and participate in the life of the people he called "savages." We know better now than to judge in that manner, but in his time the culture and society of the industrious white men of the East was the standard against which he measured. He was also able to respect and admire the noble, free men he encountered in the wilderness and to give us a vivid account of how they lived.

Francis set out to learn about the native people of the West. Despite every obstacle, especially being sick, he persevered in that goal. The trail provided to Francis the means for succeeding in his quest for discovery of the true nature of the native people.

There are great contrasts between Kit, Josiah, Uncle Dick, and Francis. They were motivated by very different reasons to travel the Santa Fe Trail. Each man had different skills and gave us different views of the West in the nineteenth century. We can synthesize their accounts and truly expand our understanding of their times and contributions.

6

SUSAN SHELBY MAGOFFIN
ON THE TRAIL TO LOVE AND WOMANHOOD

SUSAN SHELBY MAGOFFIN WAS a brave young woman who traveled the trail in 1846. She kept a diary that gives us a rare woman's point of view about the Santa Fe Trail. She was a bright, observant lady who had a unique opportunity to make the trip in relative luxury—allowing us to view the journey through very different eyes.

Susan was born July 30, 1827, into a wealthy family in Kentucky. Her family was one of prominent men, heroes, and pioneers. Isaac Shelby, her grandfather, was the first governor of Kentucky. Her youth was spent in a pampered, secure atmosphere of love and comfort, and she was well educated by tutors.

Susan Shelby Magoffin
(PD-US)

In early June 1846, she had been married to a successful Santa Fe trader, Samuel Magoffin, for eight months. When Samuel planned to set out across the Santa Fe Trail to trade in Santa Fe, New Mexico, and Chihuahua, Mexico, Susan decided to go along on an adventurous honeymoon. Samuel was Susan's senior by twenty-seven years, but the eighteen-year-old Susan was very much in love with her tall Kentuckian. She regarded his career of a frontier merchant as both hazardous and romantic.

Fortunately for us, Susan kept an informative diary of her journey, later published as *Down the Santa Fe Trail and into Mexico*, providing us with a feminine perspective on an excursion made mostly by males. In fact, she was one of the first American woman to travel the trail.

She loved to explore the countryside at every opportunity. However, there were times when she could not wander far, due to the threat of Indian attack. There were also discomforts from dust, wind and rain, rough roads, and illness, but, all in all, she was an enthused tourist who chronicled her many insights of life on the trail and the people she met.

On several occasions, soldiers heading west to the war with Mexico, which began that year, accompanied the caravan and also provided protection. Susan wrote about many social occasions where she visited with and got to know some of the highest-ranking officers as well as some of the less prestigious. Several times the wagon train was stopped by the army until it could be determined if it was safe to travel further into Mexico toward Santa Fe. Thus Susan's diary not only provides an element of the feminine viewpoint but, in addition, the effects of the war on civilian travel.

The Magoffins departed from Independence, Missouri, on June 11, and Susan excitedly declared that prairie life was beginning. They joined their wagons with those of several other traders for additional security as they approached the edge of the plains and

Indian country. Susan related how there were mules and oxen everywhere. The racket of teamsters cracking whips and gathering the animals, the noise of the lowing cattle and the braying mules, and the yelling of the men made for a novel experience. She found the swearing of the teamsters disturbing, though. Her rather puritanical religious views were often put to the test of endurance when she encountered profanity. At first she was also offended by not keeping the Sabbath holy while traveling on Sunday. However, she got used to that in time, understanding the necessity of it.

In Samuel's portion of the train were fourteen big wagons with six yokes of oxen each, one baggage wagon with two yokes of oxen, and one two-mule carriage for Susan's maid. Two mules similarly pulled Susan's carriage. Then there were two men on mules driving the extra stock of nineteen oxen, two riding horses and three extra mules. Finally, the superintendent of the wagons came along with his mule. The livestock included also Susan's dog, Ring. By Susan's count, they had twenty teamsters and three Mexican tent servants, plus herself and her maid, Jane—not the typical entourage.

When the train was thirty miles west of Independence, Susan described with great enthusiasm her new tent home. Her youthful excitement for this grand adventure with her new husband bubbles up through her writing. They were camped at a spot known as Lone Elm, because an elm tree was the only vegetation in sight, other than grass. There was sufficient water for the people and the livestock, a major motivation for choosing any campsite. Their roomy tent was designed and made in Philadelphia by a military tent maker. She described the table that hung from the central tent pole, their bed with linens, and their carpeted floor. Susan thought their meal of fried eggs, ham, and biscuits, was first-rate fare. A night of sweet rest topped off her contentment with the beginning of her safari. Due to Samuel's wealth, Susan enjoyed unique accommodations that few others could afford.

At the ninety-five mile mark from Independence, Susan passionately described the extraordinary freedom she felt and the purity of life in the outdoors. It compared very favorably to the oppression she experienced in gossiping circles back home. It is interesting that other young travelers on the trail talked about the same sense of the complete, uncomplicated freedom while roaming outside settled society. This is a theme that repeats itself, along with enthusiasm for the beauty of the country.

At their seventh campsite, Susan met her first Indian when a hungry Kaw entered the camp. He sat quietly smoking his pipe while dinner was being prepared. Then he ate his fill, and with his rifle, horse, and dog—his sole companions—he continued to roam the plains in his isolated lifestyle. Susan was impressed that he wore nothing but a breach clout. Coming from the East, she was not used to men wandering around without clothes. This was the first of many cultural shocks she would encounter as she traveled among less restrictive societies.

That same night, some of the delight of sleeping in the wilderness was marred by the racket of wolves howling near her tent. Sleep did not come so easily with those creatures' proximity, but when her dog Ring flew out of the tent and gave chase, she was much reassured of her safety. Relieved of her worries about wolves, she returned to her battle against the swarms of mosquitoes that attacked persistently all night. Luxurious travel simply could not eliminate all the discomforts.

At 145 miles from Independence, or camp nine, they arrived at Council Grove. This was a rendezvous point for groups heading west. Here they could join up in larger numbers for safety, as it was considered hostile territory farther on. There was a good supply of water for livestock and oak, hickory, and walnut trees to be cut down for timbers and wagon tongues. They would rest their stock at this stopover and make repairs to equipment before journeying into the plains. The men made bullets and prepared their firearms. It was a good first opportunity to wash some clothes, something that didn't happen often.

Susan, who loved to roam beyond their campsites, now began to feel that a hostile Indian or a wolf could be lurking behind any bush, so she stayed closer to the caravan.

As with many of our young travelers on the trail west, she had the opportunity to meet Captain Charles Bent, who was on his way east (see Chapter 1). He was famous as an early trader and was a partner of Ceran St. Vrain. Both men were very successful traders.

Leaving Council Grove, Susan described the size and diversity of their company. Americans, Mexicans, and Negroes made up the human component. There were hundreds of horses, mules, and oxen, dozens of wagons and carriages. She wrote that the camp looked like a village.

When heavy thunderstorms rolled across the prairie, as they often did, Susan explained the difficulty of moving wagons through the mud. Wheels became so mired that several teams could hardly move a wagon. On one day, she said they averaged no more than one mile an hour. When they made camp, there was neither wood for fires nor water for man or beast. The night was spent hungry and in wet clothes. Most of us can hardly imagine living in that kind of discomfort today. On another occasion, eleven yoke of oxen could not move a stuck wagon. When they were done whipping the oxen till they finally moved the wagon, the oxen had bloody necks from the yokes rubbing, and their heads and backs had whip marks. Susan felt sympathy for the hardships of the animals that got so little sympathy from the men.

When rainstorms didn't batter them, the oppressive heat took its turn. Susan admired one young driver when his ox was overcome with the heat. He saved the animal by plastering him in cooling mud and pouring water down his mouth. Susan thought he was a kind-hearted young man, though she doesn't seem to have made any effort to talk to him.

Bugs also caused a lot of the nuisance on the trail. Susan found green bugs, mosquitoes, and snakes the peskiest companions of the prairie. She was truly learning how to live close to the land, unprotected by a sumptuous house.

When one of the Mexican men in the wagon train died of consumption, Susan felt sad that only the day before he had eaten with relish the soup she sent him, and now he was dead. He was wrapped in a blanket and buried deep enough to prevent wolves from getting to him. Often the animals were driven over a grave or were corralled over a grave at night, so that they trampled the ground to prevent detection by wolves or Indians. The sadness of the burials in unmarked, lonesome graves, without anyone to care or mourn, touched many of the settlers along the trail.

When they reached the Arkansas River, Susan felt homesick, looking at the muddy waterway. It reminded her of the Mississippi. She said that even though the

Mississippi wasn't near her home, it seemed like a near neighbor compared to the three hundred miles she now was from Independence. Leaving her family and familiar surroundings to be with a new husband in a faraway place was at times, no doubt, unsettling for this young woman, but she didn't refrain from writing about the ups and downs she experienced on the long trek.

On July 4, Susan, Jane, and Samuel stayed behind when the other wagons left camp. Susan wanted to see the "wonderful curiosity" known as Pawnee Rock where hundreds of previous travelers had carved their names in the granite. Because they felt vulnerable to Indian attack when in such small numbers, Susan had Samuel and Jane stand guard while she carved her name in the rock. She said it wasn't well done because she was trembling and hurried from fear of the Indians.

Later the same day Susan and Samuel had a scare when their carriage crashed going down an embankment at the Ash Creek Crossing. Susan was stunned, but she credited Samuel with saving her. He protected her with his own body. She could have been more badly hurt, and when she saw the mess of the wreckage, she understood how disastrous the affair might have been. She felt the vulnerability that injury in the wilds imposed.

The war with Mexico also gave rise to feelings of insecurity. On July 5, the wagon train was stopped at Pawnee Fork by order of the government. The caravan of seventy-five or eighty wagons of merchandise was to wait for US troops to protect them against attack by the Mexican military. From that time until they finally arrived in Santa Fe, there was always much worry about their safety because of the lack of communications about the progress of the war.

While they waited, most of the men hunted buffalo and came back with large amounts of fat meat to dry for later in the trip, when wild life would be scarce. Susan was delighted with the dinner of buffalo hump ribs, declaring she had never eaten the equal of this meat in the finest restaurants of New York and Philadelphia. She enjoyed another fine meal as they neared Bent's Fort (now in southeastern Colorado), when they dined on "two roasted ducks and baked beans." Susan called it a splendid dinner, better than what many in the States would be eating. She was learning Spanish from people around her, so she also called the dinner "dos patos asado y frijoles cocido."

A few days later, they received permission to advance to Bent's Fort on the Arkansas River and there to await more troops for their protection. They were 180 miles from the fort. Colonel Kearny was the commanding officer of the troops that were on their way. They had no idea how long they would be kept waiting at Bent's Fort before proceeding toward Santa Fe. Of course, the traders saw these delays as a loss of earnings and were anxious about progress.

Susan rode horseback for the first time as they left for the fort. She enjoyed it, but she found that her buffalo horse had very rough gaits. She felt her riding skills had diminished since she had ridden when she was younger, but riding added a nice extra measure of that freedom she so enjoyed.

Susan felt ill on the way to Bent's Fort, and she found it terrifying to be sick on the plains. There was a doctor available to her, however, who was traveling with the army—Dr. Masure, a Frenchman. Susan had confidence in his skills, since he was known to be an excellent physician, especially with female cases. It gave her comfort to see him. She also appreciated the nursing competence of her servant Jane and the solicitous attentions of Samuel. She was a brave young lady to deal with what was an early stage of pregnancy.

All our travelers on the trail spoke repeatedly of the violent thunderstorms that blew in rapidly. On one occasion, Samuel and Susan were awakened, shortly after retiring, to raging wind, thunder, and lightning. Before Samuel could get Susan moved to one of the wagons, their tent collapsed. She was tangled in ropes and the center pole of the tent. Ultimately, she was able to shelter in Jane's carriage, as she had done after the July 4th accident.

From July 21 to 27, Susan did not write in her diary. In her next entry, she explained that the rest of the trip into Bent's Fort had been fairly uneventful, even though they saw worrisome Indian signs.

The fort was a busy, noisy place with soldiers, traders, Indians, and Mexicans loafing or preparing for further travel—all making a chaotic scene. Susan mentioned that the well in the center of the fort provided good water, especially with the luxury of rare ice that was offered. So there were some amenities available. Her description of the layout of the fort and the people working and living there is a painting in words of things that are hard to imagine now.

In her imaginative way, Susan said the fort met exactly her idea of what an ancient castle looked like. It was built of adobe, with an entrance on the east side. The thick exterior wall encircled a courtyard with a well in the center that serviced the twenty-five rooms lining the interior of the wall. The dirt floors of the rooms were sprinkled regularly with water, to hold the dust down. There was a shared dining room, a kitchen, a store, a blacksmith's shop, a barber's room, and an icehouse. There was also an enclosure for keeping some of the stock in at night, to prevent theft.

Young philosopher that she was, Susan commented that where men live there is gambling, and that was true of the fort. There was a billiard table, a racetrack, and the cackling chickens suggested to her the possibility of cockfights. In their own room, a real luxury, the furnishings were sparse—a bed, chairs, washbasin, and table. There was a common room used as a parlor.

Susan mentioned her ill health and the doctor's continuing visits. She had hoped that the travel would be beneficial to her health, but that wasn't the case. On her nineteenth birthday, she expressed alarm because she was so sick and had to stay in bed most of the time. It was a difficult place for her to rest because of the constant noise of shoeing horses, neighing and braying animals, crying children, and scolding and fighting among the men.

A room representative of Susan Shelby Magoffin's room at Bent's Fort (Bent's Old Fort National Historic Site)

On August 6, she wrote in her diary about losing her baby. She truly suffered this loss. Both she and Samuel would have been pleased to have the baby. It is hard to imagine how painful this experience was for Susan. Being so young, with no women of her family to help and comfort her, she must have missed home very much. Her unexpected initiation into womanhood and maturity called on her inner strength.

At this same time, an Indian woman in the room below Susan delivered a baby that was healthy. Within half an hour, the lady took her infant to the river and bathed with it. Susan found it impressive that this practice of "heathens" surpassed the treatment of "civilized" life, and she thought maybe society women were too careful.

Susan may have suffered the miscarriage due to the accident at Ash Creek on July 4, although there is speculation that she suffered from a condition known as Eclampsia, which can be treated today.

The common area in the center of Bent's Fort (Bent's Old Fort National Historic Site) Susan Shelby Magoffin commented on the fresh water from the well in the center of the inner fort.

As she passed the time in her bed recovering, Susan pondered the wickedness of men. She felt that waging war on each other was the act of dumb brutes. Watching Colonel Kearny and his troops prepare to leave for Santa Fe and California to wage war with Mexico triggered these thoughts for her. But after the soldiers and traders left for Santa Fe, she found the fort a desolate place.

On August 8, Samuel's wagon train left the fort, continuing toward Santa Fe and traveling only six miles that day. When they crossed the Arkansas River and left the United States, entering a foreign territory, Susan had deep feelings of patriotism about departing her homeland. There was uncertainty in her voice about leaving all she loved and going into the unknown, not knowing if she would ever return. No doubt this young woman had some reasons for missing home and security, but she leaned heavily on her faith and her love for her new husband.

The wagon train traveled distances based on where they could find water and grass. Sometimes it was twelve or fifteen miles between sources of water. At the camp known as "Hole in the Rock," their oxen took "French leave" and departed during the night. Susan commented that the only way they could have resumed their journey was if they had pulled the wagons themselves. Thirty-four head of cattle were found as far away as fifteen miles, while others were recovered closer to camp. Losing livestock was a constant danger to be guarded against.

By the 13th, they were approaching Raton Pass, a difficult fifteen-mile cut through the mountains. In the evenings, Susan liked to ramble from camp and enjoy the beautiful scenery, while still being visible to the train. Her faithful dog, Ring, stayed close by her and made her feel safe from Indians, bears, panthers, and wolves—all of which she dreaded.

Going through the pass at Raton was very difficult for wagons. One turned over and caused a delay for repairs. Susan enjoyed walking that day and hoped the exercise was beneficial. On the 14th, Susan was thrilled with the magnificent vistas. She liked to explore the streams and to roam on the hillsides. She said that they were traveling at one-half mile per hour as the road grew worse and worse. She rode her horse the next day, delighted to be on horseback and continuing to enjoy the views. Another day, she and Jane climbed to the top of a mountain, where she could see the village of Mora in the valley below. She found that spot peaceful and wondered if she would want to live there, though she felt strong ties to family and friends left behind. As a female, Susan seemed much more open to sharing her thoughts and feelings along the trail than the young men who left their journals. She is much more introspective. It is wonderful to see the land through her eyes.

An express communication from General Kearny was received about whether they would be able to

Mora Valley, where Susan Shelby Magoffin found such peace

enter Santa Fe—the city was under the control of the Mexicans. Samuel's brother, James, had gone ahead to negotiate with the Mexican General Armijo about letting the traders enter the city. Susan said that James had the confidence of the generals and they expected good results from his negotiations. If they had to turn back, they would at least be the first in the retreat line, since they were last among the wagon trains.

As they waited for wagon repairs, Susan enjoyed another climb up the mountain. She said she would miss the mountains when they again entered the plains. It took five days to exit Raton pass. Susan felt sad that she wouldn't be able to continue riding her horse, as the plains were too hot. However, she later commented that the August temperatures were more like October, and the nights were cold.

On August 26, they arrived in Las Vegas, New Mexico, a small Mexican settlement that Susan called the village of Vegas. It was quite an experience for her. She felt like she was a sideshow because of the crowds that gathered and pressed upon her. Small children, half-clothed or naked, stared at her with mouths agape. She had to suppress laughter at their wonder. When Susan was taken into a room to get something to eat, the crowd followed her and continued gawking.

Preparation for serving a meal involved a white cloth laid over a table and then a dirty, greasy cloth laid on top, which was more brown than white. A soup of meat, green peppers, and onion was then served without eating utensils. The food was wrapped in a tortilla, but Susan couldn't really eat much of the spicy food that she was unaccustomed to. She was better able to eat some corn and a fried egg that were served. She was relieved to return as soon as possible to her carriage and again be alone and free of the people staring at her.

Typical of Americans riding into that area of New Mexico, Susan was shocked at what seemed to her to be the loose ways of the women. She commented on their bare arms and necks and their exposed bosoms. To cross the streams, these women pulled their dresses, which only went to their calves to start with, above their knees and splattered through the water. She had to keep her veil up around her face to cover her blushing!

On August 27, they received news that Governor Armijo had fled Santa Fe and General Kearny had secured the town for the United States. This was good news. They would be able to have a break in Santa Fe before progressing into Mexico on business.

Near the village of Pecos, Susan visited the ruins of the Pecos Pueblo. When Coronado visited the area in 1540, there were about twenty-five hundred inhabitants. She was quite awed by the building that had gone on, both in the ancient pueblo dwellings and in the church built by the early Spanish settlers. She felt sad to ride over what once had been a thriving community. It was a poignant experience for her to visit this disappeared civilization.

Ruins of the church built by the Spanish at the Pecos Ruins (Pecos National Historic Park)

From Pecos, the caravan would arrive in Santa Fe within a day. Susan was relieved at that news. However, on August 30, 1846, the Magoffins reached town at such a late hour that Susan was unable to form an impression of the town. She was quite amazed to wake up the next morning in a place where only a short time ago it would have seemed folly to try to visit. She was in exotic Santa Fe! Susan felt a surge of pride at being the first American woman to arrive there.

It wasn't acceptable for her to explore alone, being a woman, so she had to gain her impressions from the little she could see. She described that the town was in a valley and had a large church, a central plaza, and a river flowing through it.

General Kearny had taken the city and placed himself in the governor's chair. He raised the American flag and made Santa Fe part of the United States, but he had not molested the people in any way. He asked for their allegiance and allowed them their way of life. They had feared that he would outlaw their Catholic religion, but, compatible with the philosophy of separation of church and state, he made no attempt to do that. Rumors and fears about how the people would be treated by the conquerors turned out to be unfounded. Others worried that the Mexican Army would return and recapture the city. When communications were so poor, hearsay formed the basis of "news," and sometimes speculation ran rampant.

Susan was delighted with their four-room house, and she was pleased to finally be able to set up a real home for herself and Samuel. She wanted to prove herself a capable mistress of a well-run home, and she set about accomplishing that. They enjoyed the company of Samuel's brother, James, as they re-united before he was to leave shortly for Mexico, ahead of General Kearny.

Susan became preoccupied with "callers" on an almost daily basis. She returned many "calls" and enjoyed the social life. On days without visitors, she was disappointed. After all, at that time a proper girl just didn't go out and wander around on her own. She must have missed the freedom of her rides in the mountains. A day could be confining while she stayed home alone and Samuel was out on business.

She never hesitated to record her impressions of people, and she particularly enjoyed General Kearny and his attentions to her. It was especially fun when he took her on a riding tour of Fort Marcy and the vicinity. She thought it was good that General Kearny had not had to fight his way through the canyon and that he was able to take the city without a fight. Her position in relation to people in high places allowed her to form such opinions.

Susan enjoyed her housekeeping and was rather proud of the results. She learned a lot of the Spanish language and how to make purchases without getting cheated by the locals. She grew very fond of a little girl who called to sell her produce, being impressed with the child's manners and confidence. She also loved the dry climate of New Mexico and the clean, clear air of the high elevation.

After attendance at her first fandango, a local dance, she delighted in writing about the evening. She reviewed who attended, what they wore, what the music was like, and how they behaved. She enjoyed the attentions of the young officers who were serving in the victorious army.

Being very sociable, Susan never tired of recording many details, including her personal views. She commented that, at one dinner they were invited to attend, she didn't like the custom that men and women were seated separately. Another practice that displeased her occurred during the local Catholic services, when the music—played on a violin and guitar that were constantly being tuned—included the same songs heard at the fandango the night before. To a Protestant raised in the strictest piety, to even think of a dance tune in church would have been outrageous. To actually hear one was shocking!

When the newly appointed local officials and the merchants gave a ball for the general and his corps, Susan lavished her diary with descriptions of what people wore, how the Governor's Palace was appointed, and what the dances were like. All the ladies danced and smoked "cigarritas," small cigars of tobacco rolled in corn husks. Women smoking in public were pretty scandalous, but Susan observed her new culture more than she made judgments about it.

On October 2, they received news that peace had been made with Mexico. Now they could prepare to continue their trip to Chihuahua for Samuel's trading business. When they commenced traveling south, the journey continued to be fraught with uncertainty about their safety and what was really going on between Mexico and the United States. News remained very unreliable.

Susan's journal ended nearly a year later, on September 8, 1847. While still traveling in Mexico, she suffered from yellow fever and she lost a baby boy. The Magoffins returned to Kentucky in 1848. Susan's health had been damaged by the hardships she had endured. She had a baby girl in 1855, but Susan died soon after on October 16, 1855. It is sad to think that she died so young and never had the chance to raise any of her babies. Unlike many others though, she did survive the trip across the prairie on the Santa Fe Trail.

As an inexperienced young woman, Susan set out on a romantic trip with her new husband, probably not realizing what she was really getting into. But she adapted, grew, and learned about the world around her. For Susan, the trail led to experiencing a strong love that supported her through difficult times. Samuel Magoffin inspired that love in her. With the loss of her baby, she now knew what womanhood really meant.

Like our other travelers on the Santa Fe Trail, Susan initially expressed the common prejudices of the time toward Indians and Mexicans. But like most open-minded, enthused wanderers of the world, she set aside her concepts of their primitiveness and adapted her views when she came to know the people better. Susan was open, curious, and detailed in her reporting of what she saw.

Her diary provides us with feminine insights colored by the culture and mores of the time that she came from. It is a wonderful addition to the many chronicles left to us by the young men who traveled the trail in the same years.

7

HECTOR LEWIS GARRARD
ON THE TRAIL TO MANHOOD

Hector Lewis Garrard (known as Lewis Garrard), a seventeen-year-old Cincinnatian from an affluent family, set out to see the West during the Mexican War (1846). As a very young man, he had already traveled down the Mississippi River, along the Gulf Coast to Texas, and back to the Louisiana coast. He had ventured forth in February 1846 and stayed with friends in Louisiana until May of that year. He enjoyed visiting friends, riding horses, and shooting the alligators and ducks of the swamps.

When he returned home from the South, he was bitten by an urge to travel and see the West, as a result of having read John C. Fremont's report of his explorations in the Rocky Mountains in 1842–43. He persuaded his parents to allow him to undertake a phenomenal adventure for a seventeen-year-old. They provided him with letters of credit, cash, a Bible, and a rifle. In July he took a low-water steamer to St. Louis, Missouri. Travel by such a steamer was a miserable experience, with sweltering heat, delays from running aground on sandbars, little sleep, and poor food.

Upon arriving in St. Louis, he traversed the teeming streets, after having left his baggage with a hotel porter, and made his way to the Planter's House Hotel, where he found accommodations. St. Louis was a busy port of embarkation for the West. The city was a trading center where throngs of people busily conducted the work necessary to the booming business of wagon train trade to points west as well as river commerce north and south.

Lewis received letters of introduction from Mr. Kenneth McKenzie at the Pierre Chouteau Jr. & Co. offices. The company ran numerous trading forts in the Indian territory. Lewis found the gentlemen to whom he was introduced very helpful in his preparations for the trip. Like Francis Parkman, Lewis would travel as a tourist, but in contrast, he would not have the same kind of purpose that Francis had, that of making a study. Lewis was a young man with a drive to see the world. He kept a journal, writing almost daily of his expedition at the request of his older brothers, who wanted him to record events of interest. Throughout his journey, through sickness and arduous conditions, Lewis maintained an observant and sensitive record of his journey—an impressive feat for someone so young.

Fortunately, Mr. Ceran St. Vrain, of the firm Bent, St. Vrain & Co., famous Santa Fe traders (see Chapter 1), was also staying at the Planter's House Hotel. He was preparing a train to go west, and he invited Lewis along. Everyone recognized that traveling in numbers added to security. He also requested that Lewis join his "mess." That meant Lewis would be part of a small group that would camp together and share their meals and campfire. Lewis had good connections.

After touring the St. Louis area and purchasing supplies like caps and powder, Lewis set out for Kansas via the Missouri River. He traveled alone on this leg of the journey, but made friends easily, and he enjoyed shooting ducks with young men he met along the way. He ran into Mr. T. B. Drinker, a former editor of the Cincinnati newspaper, with whom he spent his waiting time until Mr. St. Vrain arrived at the meeting place near Westport. From there, the plan was to cross the plains to Bent's Fort in what is now Colorado with Mr. St. Vrain's wagon train. Eventually Lewis's travels took him to the area of the Spanish Peaks in Colorado and the Taos trail in New Mexico. The Spanish Peaks were a landmark for navigation in southern Colorado.

Lewis was an energetic young man with a keen eye for observation. He and Mr. Drinker made camp and then explored the area. Lewis observed the local Indians and felt saddened by the manner in which the liquor traders took advantage of them. The traders were very destructive, causing the Indians to become dependent on alcohol for the gain of the traders. The Indians were ill prepared to avoid the dangers of intoxication. They would trade everything they had for this brew and were degraded into terrible poverty.

In September, Mr. St. Vrain arrived, and final preparations for departure were undertaken. For fifty dollars, Lewis bought a spotted horse that was noted as a "buffalo chaser," which he unoriginally named Paint.

Lewis observed and wrote about how cruel some of the handling of livestock was and how hard the travel was for the animals. He felt that only the toughest of mules could survive the teamsters' method for breaking the animals to harness. They were lassoed and tied short to a wagon wheel without food for twenty-four hours, to take the fight out of them. Then they were harnessed to a heavy wagon and lashed until they pulled.

After an hour's confusion and fighting, those mules that were uninjured gave in and were considered broken to harness.

On September 12, 1846, a late date in the travel season for departure, the wagon train was finally ready to set out. Lewis painted a wonderful word picture of the sights and sounds, the hustle and bustle of the departure. The to and fro of the wagons in a rutted trail, the shouts of the drivers of the oxen, the efforts of the herders of the *caballada* (herd of horses and mules), all contributed to the excitement and the sense of an adventure underway. The riders reached their first camp by dark, but the slower oxen-drawn wagons continued arriving until late at night.

This was a very exciting undertaking for a seventeen-year-old boy, and Lewis described what he saw in a manner that even now can take us back to that night. Their camp had wood, grass, and water, which were the three things the scouts searched for in campsites. It took a lot of grass to feed their huge herds of mules, horses, and oxen each night. Since they were still in an area that had trees, they could burn a nice fire to cook over. Water was an essential that became scarcer as they moved into the plains, but early campsites were comfortable.

However, by September 16, a hard rain that came down all day brought an awareness of some of the discomforts to come. Because the wagons were full of trade goods, the men slept on the ground, wrapped in a blanket. By morning, Lewis's blanket and clothes were soaked through, and he shivered with cold. As a young adventurer, Lewis was beginning to learn that this trip would not be luxurious.

Lewis introduced us to several fellow travelers who would become his friends. Most important was Mr. St.

Vrain, whom he described as an experienced mountain man and trader. But he also said Mr. St. Vrain was a true gentleman who spoke with honesty and politeness. These were traits that would not always be apparent among some of the rough-cut men Lewis would travel with later. He was always grateful to Mr. St. Vrain as a considerate mentor from whom he learned a lot on the way to Bent's Fort.

Included in Lewis's mess were an Indian trader, the wagon master, a company clerk, Mr. Drinker, and a couple of others. Lewis found them a very agreeable and helpful group—something that must have been reassuring to the young man, as they took him under their wing.

When Lewis met the men of the wagon train, he commented on how much he enjoyed the French Canadian men from St. Louis, who were the team drivers. He found them always congenial and full of high spirits, despite the trials and tribulations of the trail. In the evenings, they would often sing songs in their native tongue. Lewis found their beautiful songs pleasing to the ear, even though he did not understand the language. Throughout the trip, he enjoyed the company of these exuberant men, perhaps because they mirrored his own enthusiasm to jump in and try every experience that would teach him about the West and the people who lived there.

On September 30, they arrived at Council Grove, on the edge of the last timbered land with abundant water. From here, the grass became less luxurious, water more scarce, and danger from Indian encounters more likely. After they left this area, their only campfire fuel would be the dung of the buffalo. Piles of it had to be gathered at each camp, but this new fuel burned quite adequately.

Being a greenhorn, Lewis had to learn to lasso his horse in the mornings. Paint unfortunately had many tricks for avoiding the lasso, and on the first morning out of Council Grove, Lewis was unable to catch the pony. He walked with the entertaining French Canadian drivers who, rain or shine, hungry or satisfied, were always easy-going and pleasant company. The drivers of the wagons walked beside the oxen and commanded them with words and the use of the bullwhip. Imagine walking from Council Grove in Kansas to Bent's Fort in what is now southeastern Colorado. Of course, at that time neither Kansas nor Colorado existed as a state; each was part of the Indian territory. Presumably, Lewis's lassoing skills improved so he could ride.

All the members of the train were only able to eat twice a day, and sometimes there was only one meal in twenty-four hours. Men were often hungry, and they looked forward with great anticipation to the time when they would start seeing herds of buffalo and be able to improve their fare. Buffalo meat was a staple of the trail, and Lewis found it a very satisfying meat.

Hunting buffalo was very exciting and always dangerous. A wounded bull would often turn on a rider and charge his horse. A herd had to be approached with care in order to avoid stampeding them before the hunters were within firing range. On one occasion, a hunter saw a blind bull and decided to add some fresh meat to the evening meal. He crawled up close to the animal, and the bull sensed his presence by smell but could not see where he was. It charged here and there in an effort to find him. When the hunter fired, the animal was directed to him by the sound of the shot and took chase. The hunter, yelling with fear, ran for the wagons, with the blind animal in close pursuit. Fortunately one of the teamsters was able to shoot the bull before it made its kill.

The buffalo herds were always attended by packs of wolves that were constantly on the prowl for weakened animals. At one time, Lewis saw a herd being chased by a pack of wolves that he estimated at two hundred or more large wolves.

On October 13, the wagon train reached a landmark called Pawnee Rock, in what is now west-central Kansas. The Rock was thirty-five or forty feet tall. The soft sandstone offered a site where many people carved their names, to leave a record for future generations that they had traveled the Santa Fe Trail.

Lewis climbed to the top of Pawnee Rock, where he found the remains of someone who had died there. He found it particularly poignant that this fellow, and so many others who got sick on the trail, was jolted about in a wagon during the scorching heat, only to die in such a lonely place. To be put in a mere hole, wrapped in a blanket as shroud and coffin, without any dear one to mourn, seemed to him a very difficult fate. Of course, there was no way of knowing why this man died up on the rock. For a seventeen-year-old boy who was tough enough to live this trail life, Lewis was very sensitive to the vagaries of life. We see a picture being painted of thoughtfulness and caring. He was an observer of life's nuances. These qualities continue to show up in his journal.

On October 16, they awoke with a very cold "norther" blowing. They rode with all their extra clothes on. Lewis explained how they kept comfortable at night: They had their saddles and overcoats as a pillow and slept in their clothes. The men decided to sleep in twos to share warmth on a pallet of buffalo robes, with the little bit of heat provided by the buffalo chip fires.

The caravan arrived on October 23 at the Cimarron crossing of the Arkansas River, where they had two options. The shorter but more difficult route was the Cimarron Route that went across a long distance of desert where water was very scarce. The other choice was to continue following the river to Bent's Fort and then cross a spur of the Rocky Mountains over the Raton Pass. That was the longer but safer and easier route in terms of water supply. In this case, Bent's Fort was the destination.

At the crossing of the Arkansas, Lewis forded the river to visit with a party he saw on the other side. These men were a party of four, riding as government express couriers. Whenever travelers encountered each other on the trail, they were anxious to exchange whatever news they had. It could be a long, lonely journey, where individuals were cut off from any account of what was going on in the world. Weather, Indian activity, wagon trains on the trail, deaths, and more were the bits of information that were sought. Amazingly, news passing from group to group reached long distances.

Lewis often commented on the thrilling feeling of riding a fleet horse, with a trusty rifle across the saddle, the wind blowing in his hair. He found the openness and freedom of the plains very exhilarating. When a traveler who was headed east offered to buy his trusty Paint, he declined without response. He said he thought about how he valued Paint and the true liberty that they were sharing. This was a recurring theme with all our travelers.

Two Cheyenne Indians came into camp on October 24. These were the first "wild Indians" that Lewis had seen. He described their nakedness, except for a loincloth, moccasins, and a robe around their shoulders, which dropped to their waists when they rode. While they ate and talked, they found that the Indians were runners for a large war party of Cheyennes that numbered about 122 warriors and were camped up the river. They were on a scalp- and horse-stealing expedition against the Pawnee Indians.

When Lewis visited the Cheyenne camp and watched the younger braves dashing around on their splendid horses, he thought with envy of the free and happy life that they lived on the open plains. They had buffalo to provide for their needs and fine horses to ride. He believed they were part of a wild and lovely nature, living and dying in ignorance of worries. It must have been exciting at his age to see such an unfettered existence.

One evening when rain fell and the wind blew, the men curled up in their blankets early to sleep. Lewis, as usual, stayed up to read or write in his journal, or to dream of friends far away. However, he awoke in the morning drenched and cold. On an empty stomach, he hastily joined a couple of others to ride ahead to Bent's Fort, forty miles away. He felt strongly motivated to cover the forty miles to reach safety, food, some comfort, and a new phase of his adventure.

After a weary day of trotting his horse endlessly, he finally reached the fort, pulled the saddle off, and turned his pony loose to fend for itself on local grass and water. For the first time in fifty days, he sat at a table for dinner and used knife, fork, and plate to eat. That was a luxurious change after eating off a dirty saddle blanket spread on the ground.

Lewis was detailed in his physical description of the fort. He appreciated the beauty of the view of the Spanish Peaks, a landmark of renown. The fort was peopled by an interesting diversity—traders, employers, government officers and their men, Indians, Frenchmen, and hunters. He made the acquaintance of a Lieutenant Buchanan, who had left the army to see New Mexico.

On November 8, Lewis joined a trader named John Smith and traveled with him, his Cheyenne wife, and their little boy to a Cheyenne village for trading. The Indian etiquette dictated that the first lodge that a stranger entered had to provide hospitality to the visitor as long as he stayed. Lewis and John Smith deliberately asked for, and then entered, the lodge of Lean Chief, for he was friendly and welcoming. The visitors took the position of importance at the back of the lodge, while family members moved to allow them the place of honor.

Then the Indians and Lewis's party followed Indian customs of welcome. First, they were given water to drink. Then meat was offered to them. Only after smoking a pipe together could they satisfy each other's curiosity and share news. Lewis admired the Indians' forbearance, because they were as curious as anyone for information, but first they cared for their guest's comfort. Lewis and John Smith contributed coffee to the meal. It was a favored extravagance for the Indians and they enjoyed it heartily.

The next morning, the tribe decided to move the village. Lewis was enthralled by the immediate commotion of moving a whole village. Young men drove the bands of horses. Women took down the poles of the lodges and bundled them to form a travois that the horses could pull. Small children rode on top of the buffalo-skin tepees that made up the travois covering. Tools were put in skin bags and packed on mules. Everyone and everything was in motion.

Lewis watched from a vantage point. Organized chaos reigned. The initial four or five lodges were followed by the trader's wagon. Young boys gamboled about on their horses, herding the livestock or just dashing around for amusement. The animals pulling the travois jogged along without regard for rough ground, bouncing their small, wide-eyed, laughing passengers. Young maidens rode on their beautiful horses in their best buckskin dresses, which were high at the neck, sleeveless, and knee-length. From the knees down, they wore leggings that terminated in a moccasin. Their unconfined life and free-spirited riding was much admired by Lewis, but he hastened to add that modesty would prevent ladies of the East from wearing such garb. Coming from a very formal society, especially as far as the behavior of girls was concerned, it must have been a wonder to see women dressed so revealingly.

After two hours, the chiefs and elderly men dismounted to sit in a circle and smoke their pipes, a sign to the tribe that they had reached their destination. With that, the women unpacked the animals, pitched the tents, built fires, arranged the robes—in general, set up housekeeping. Then the chiefs and warriors went to their lodges to wait while the women cooked dinner. Lewis thought the men were very lazy and was provoked that they contributed nothing to the work. He felt they should be helping and more protective of the women.

Two days later, Lewis returned to Bent's Fort, but he had enjoyed being in the Cheyenne camp so much that he returned with John Smith and a load of goods to again set up trading with the Indians. He commented on how the chief doted on his six-month-old grandson and was so proud of him. The family hope was that he would be a great warrior. The girls did not get attention from the males but were raised for work and obedience.

Lewis and his party were invited to the lodge of a warrior named Gray Eyes, who had two wives and twelve children. Gray Eyes beamed with pride on two sons who were present. They were ages fifteen summers and thirteen summers. He bragged about their having killed buffalo from horseback with bow and arrow. That was dangerous work for young boys, work we would consider too dangerous, but the proud father saw them as budding and capable warriors. The Indians never chastised a boy, for they thought it would break his spirit.

This was one of the occasions when a lunch of a bowl of indeterminate meat was served, and everyone reached in and helped themselves with knives and fingers. Lewis wondered about the food that was handled and prepared by women who didn't know about washing hands.

Eating dog meat did not appeal at all to Lewis, though the mountain men told him often that it was very good. He knew that the Indians ate dog meat and considered it a delicacy. He also noted that when food was somewhat scarce, the large packs of dogs around the Indian camp would be diminished. One night, when the women were preparing dinner, the men told Lewis they were cooking terrapin and described the process of gathering and cooking the meat. When Lewis tried it, he found it quite good and he ate well. Then his friends let him know that he had just eaten dog meat. From then on, the story provided his traveling companions with much merriment, but Lewis got over his aversion and decided dog meat was second only to buffalo.

Lewis made many detailed observations about the Indians that we have rarely seen. He tried to write their language down, much to their amusement. He tried to explain pictures in a book that he carried, and the chiefs had many questions about these images, which were so incomprehensible to them. Often the Indians simply decided that the white man was foolish for the impractical things he spent time on. Their lives were about raiding and providing buffalo kills to their families for their survival needs.

Lewis also pondered over the mountain men, like John Smith. Though they sought a wilderness life because of their disenchantment with civilization and were rough, sometimes violent men, he saw under their crude exteriors that they were also full of the fun of life and were kind and obliging. He felt John Smith, who had run away from his task of learning tailoring to join a wagon train, was a good example. After wandering with several tribes, he settled down with a Cheyenne wife and became as one of them. He preferred the free life of roaming the plains in the Indian style—though it entailed serious risks.

On one occasion, Lewis and his companions encountered Arapaho warriors and had a close call with them. They were on a winter trading trip to the Cheyennes and suffering greatly from the cold. John Smith had left his rifle in the wagon because his hands were too cold to handle it. Riding well ahead of the wagon to find and break trail through the snow, John Smith and Lewis suddenly spotted about thirty riders coming toward them. When they could determine that they were Arapahos, John Smith quietly signaled alarm. Lewis discreetly placed a cap in his rifle.

They met the Indians, trying desperately to avoid showing fear, and greeted them with the standard handshake, which was received very coldly. They were told that the white man was bad, that he ran the buffalo out of the country, and starved the Arapahos. John Smith did some fast talking with sign language, explaining that he had been trading for a long time with the Cheyennes, who were brothers to the Arapaho, and that he only took the meat he needed. He pointed out his Cheyenne wife suggesting his brotherhood. He blamed the killing of the buffalo on white government men whom he had turned his back on. He lived as a Cheyenne. The Indian responded that he spoke with a forked tongue. As the Arapahos belligerently rode away, they tried to take the extra horses, but John Smith made an adroit move to ward them off.

After they left, Smith explained that the Arapahos were returning from a successful raid and had spent all their rage. However, Smith's wagon was driven by a Mexican who was somewhat in the distance, and they feared for him. When he caught up to them, he had taken quite a scare.

Lewis thought it queer that when the Indians had left, John Smith upbraided him for showing fear, when Lewis felt John Smith's pale, rigid face and twitching eyes had shown a lot of fear too. They had all had a bad fright, as they were badly outnumbered. They moved on very quickly. When Lewis and his party reached the village of their Cheyenne friends, they felt secure and relieved.

Another time, they met an elderly Indian trader, who was traveling alone. Lewis felt a great sympathy for him. He believed the man had worked hard but was alone and poor, with no source of old-age security. Once again displaying an unusual sensitivity to the plight of an individual, Lewis later wondered what had ever become of him.

Winter travel was really difficult. On one trip to William Bent's camp among the Cheyennes, the snow was a couple of feet deep. The mules and oxen were starving and exhausted from fighting through the snow, and there was nothing to eat but a one-day's supply of dried meat. Lewis decided this was the dark side of prairie life. The forty-mile trek that took two days in good weather now required five days. They arrived frozen, hungry, and spent.

On the other hand, Lewis felt that it was very satisfying to arrive in a camp, build a fire in the middle of a snowstorm, and share food and companionship with his friends, despite the knowledge that they were miles from anyone else. He did feel bad, though, for their hungry, fatigued animals that had to stand out in the cold night, too tired to forage through the deep snow for something to eat. They had to break ice for the animals just to allow them a drink. The wilderness was hard on the livestock that served men.

When they arrived at the Cheyenne camp, Lewis was very disheartened when he discovered that the maiden, Smiling Moon, whom he had a crush on, had married in his absence. However, he soon decided that there would be other fair maidens among the Cheyennes or elsewhere.

Lewis had only traveled with the clothes he had on. Over time, he determined that his pants were worn to a point where he had to make a change. He skirted the village and arrived at the lodge of the Mexican trader, where he procured buckskins for new trousers. John Smith cut the pants pattern for him, and Smith's wife sewed them with an awl. That was how it was done long before Walmart!

On January 28, 1847, Lewis was at the Big Timbers with William Bent and others when a friend arrived with the news of the Taos Rebellion (see Chapter 1). The death of Charles Bent was a crushing blow for William, who was the younger brother; he looked up to Charles as a father. Lewis felt sympathy for William and agreed to ride with him the following morning for Bent's Fort, forty miles away. There was no way to get news of whether the rebellion had taken over New Mexico or whether it had been defeated, and they feared for their safety but rode hard all day and reached the fort that night, without incident.

After a couple of days of confusion about what should be done, many men had gathered at the fort. William Bent resolved to head for Taos to see what was going on and to fight if necessary. Lewis determined to ride with the twenty-three men who set out for Taos. Incredibly, they took the boy with them. Who was to tell him he couldn't go?

Winter weather impeded their progress. At their first encampment, they awakened covered in a heavy snow and decided to stay in camp for a day to fight the cold by the fire. They subsisted on bread and coffee.

One of two pueblos at Taos. The scene of the Taos Rebellion in 1847.

En route to Taos, they met an Indian who brought the news that Colonel Price and 250 men had marched into Taos and killed 200 Mexicans and Indians. Those in the party who had families in Taos were much relieved to find out that the American soldiers had put the rebellion down. Their party headed for the ranch on the Verméjo River, where Lewis remained for a while, helping a cattleman gather his herd to inventory them. The insurgent Mexicans had driven the livestock off into the surrounding countryside.

At one point, Lewis realized he had been wearing the same shirt for forty-two days. He hadn't washed his face or combed his hair in the same amount of time. He decided to clean up and wash out his shirt in the nearby stream, but he also asked a friend who was making a return trip to the fort to bring him back three new shirts.

When Lewis finally arrived in Taos, Mr. St. Vrain invited him to stay at his home. Lewis was delighted with this hospitality and thoroughly appreciated a house, a good meal including vegetables, a table to dine on,

The scene of the Taos rebellion. The bell tower is all that is left of the church where the rebels hid.

sheets to sleep on, a good night's rest in a quiet, safe place where it was warm, and the charming company of the ladies of the house. This was luxury.

Lewis witnessed a trial of six of the participants in the rebellion. He described a court system with little or no proper procedure for the rights of the accused. Among the judges were a friend of Charles Bent and the father of a young man killed in the rebellion. Both were appointees to the New Mexico Territory Superior Court. George Bent, brother to Charles and William, was foreman of the jury. Some of the jury members were also friends of Charles Bent. Not exactly an unbiased group! Over a fifteen-day period, the court found fifteen men guilty of murder and treason, and they were sentenced to death.

This was Lewis's reaction to the trial:

> It certainly did appear to be a great assumption on the part of the Americans to conquer a country and then arraign the revolting inhabitants for treason. After an absence of a few minutes, the jury returned with a verdict of "guilty in the first degree" —five for murder, one for treason. Treason, indeed! What did the poor devil know about his new allegiance? I left the room, sick at heart. Justice! Out upon the word, when its distorted meaning is the warrant for murdering those who defend to the last their country and their homes.*

Lewis saw that the prisoners betrayed no emotion, but he sensed their anguish. There were many times that Lewis showed this kind of empathy for people and

---

* Lewis H. Garrard, *Way-to-yah and the Taos Trail* (Norman: University of Oklahoma Press, 1955), 172.

questioned the lack of justice in the proceedings of the authorities. His reaction to these trials shows how he was maturing into his manhood.

During one of the several trials, while Mrs. Bent was testifying and she identified the Indian, Tomás Romero, who had killed the Governor, the Indian showed no malice or hatred on his face for her as she sealed his death warrant. Lewis was amazed at Tomás's mastery of control over his emotions and this noble example of stoicism.

On the day of the hanging of several prisoners, which included the Mexican patriot, Lewis felt the patriot showed the true spirit of martyrdom worthy of his cause—that of the liberty of his country. The prisoner asserted his own innocence, the injustice of his trial, and the arbitrary conduct of his murderers. For so young a man, Lewis observed the world with a very discerning eye, compassion, and mature sense of justice.

When Lewis left Taos, he summarized his assessment of the people who lived there. He found the New Mexican men with little to recommend them, but he felt the women were like women the world over—kind and generous. He wrote that there was much to admire in the valley and more to condemn, but he still left with some reluctance. He had learned and experienced a lot in his time in this foreign town that was suddenly part of the United States as part of the Territory of New Mexico.

Lewis left El Valle de Taos with friends and rode to where William Bent was overseeing a herd of cattle he planned to move. Lewis helped gather the cattle and drive them to a ranch in the Purgatoire Valley, through which flowed the "River of Souls" or Purgatoire River. He found herding cattle somewhat tedious. However, they found good shelter for camp on the Verméjo River, in what is now northeastern New Mexico, with plenty of water and fuel to keep a cook fire. They had milk, bread, beef, and coffee. Lewis commented that when mountaineers had plenty to eat, they were cheerful; however, in starving times, an old bear was better company.

A country that was unattractive to many struck Lewis as having many attractions. Here, with a good mule, a gun, and faithful friends, he felt a wonderful feeling of liberty and an absence of fear. No one told him what to do. All he needed was a blanket for a home, and he could dress as he pleased. There was no need for money except to buy coffee, ammunition, and some whiskey. He and his companions were content. The freedom from the conventional rules of society that restricted other men, allowed Lewis to be whatever he wanted to be. He found a great deal of joy in that.

On one ride to Bent's Fort, it was decided to take a shortcut via Hole in the Rock. The route had no water, and by noon the sun was taking a terrible toll on man and beast. At sunset, they took a break for a smoke and then rode on for two more hours, searching for water. When they reached Hole in the Rock, they were rewarded with a puddle of warm water. They fought off the thirsty mules until the men had drunk their fill, and then the animals were allowed to drink. After fourteen hot hours in the saddle, the men drank until they felt like bursting. However, a convivial camp with plenty to eat was reward enough at the end of the day.

When Lewis finally joined a wagon train headed back to Missouri, he encountered rude American teamsters along the trail and compared them to the French Canadian drivers he had so enjoyed. He had moments of nostalgia for the mountains and the men he had known there. He was still seven hundred miles from civilization, but already he was feeling a nagging loss as he headed east.

As the wagon train set up camp, it was found that a man who had been sick had died. Lewis described how they dug a shallow hole and wrapped the man in a blanket to bury him. They knew wolves would soon find the grave. The next morning another man was found dead where he had been sleeping in a wagon. Another shallow grave was dug. Lewis felt a strong melancholy as they left these men in their vulnerable, unmarked graves on the desolate, windswept prairie, so far from friends or relatives to mourn them. When a man fell sick there was little comfort or help for him.

Many of the wagon train's members where sick with scurvy, a disease caused by their limited diet. Lewis contributed a pain-relieving medication he had, to help some of them get relief. The progressive symptoms included sore feet, then the legs contracted, and then the patient limped in pain. The victims were hungry all the time, and eventually dysentery and loss of weight killed them. Another shallow grave would be dug in the lonely prairie. The trail seemed littered with the bones of past sufferers.

On May 17, 1847, the party reached Fort Mann at the Cimarron crossing of the Arkansas River. They were now in territory claimed by the Comanche and Pawnee Indians. The government had sent Daniel P. Mann and forty teamsters to build this fort between Santa Fe and Fort Leavenworth as a station for repairing wagons and replenishing livestock. It was four log houses connected by timbers.

Six days after Lewis's arrival, a man was shot by the Comanches while fishing in the river about three hundred yards from the fort. Oxen and forty mules were run off by the yelping Indians. Everyone had to be constantly vigilant. The teamsters decided it wasn't worth it to stay there for thirty dollars a month. Finally, nine men were persuaded to stay to finish the building and to protect the fort. Since a friend of Lewis's was in charge and Lewis had not yet been in an Indian fight, nor served in the military, he decided to stay on for the adventure.

When the majority of the party left, Lewis felt some fear and loneliness. There remained ten healthy men and three sick ones to defend against hundreds of Indians. Not an encouraging prospect! Though Lewis understood that they were in a dangerous situation, he meant to keep his word to help out.

The bright light in his existence was the small son of his friend John Smith, the commander, and Smith's Indian wife. Lewis felt Little Jack contributed to his happiness despite the fact that Little Jack knew no English. The boy brought sweet memories of hearth and home to him.

Lewis always enjoyed the companionship of some of the men in his travels, and his descriptions of them help us understand some of the many reasons people traveled the Santa Fe Trail. At the fort, he mentioned Sam Caldwell, a former sailor who decided to see the country by signing up with the government as a teamster. Cain Stickler was a nineteen-year-old schoolmaster who also wanted to join in the Mexican War and worked as a teamster returning to the States. Roy was mysterious and thought to probably have been in the penitentiary. Andrew had been a principle witness in a murder case who was bribed to perjure himself with the offer of a horse and considerable money; he had no plans to return to Missouri and face jail. Rasamus Cowhorn had been in the battle of Sacramento during the Mexican

War and was returning to the States when he was hired to stay and help at the fort.

When a band of Arapahos approached the fort and wanted to be admitted to trade for whiskey, things were a little tense. They did not want the Indians to know how weak their force was, but Lewis was able to ask for a peace chief named Warratoria, with whom he was acquainted. Lewis wrote he was "filled with reverence for the old man, even though he was but an ignorant savage." The Arapahos set up their village of eighty lodges near the fort and settled in.

Later in the day, a train arrived from Santa Fe, headed east. The next day, another train came by, and more Indians showed up to trade. It is surprising how busy this isolated place could be. Lewis worked hard around the fort, making adobe bricks for improvements and cutting wood when it was safe to venture out.

Various men that Lewis knew and who passed by the fort urged him to return east with them. They felt that the small number of men to protect the fort made it a very dangerous place to be. However, Lewis remained true to his promise to help there until an old friend of his father's came through. Colonel Russell was shocked to find Lewis in this fort with only ten men to defend it. The colonel thought it was sheer madness for Lewis, who wasn't really a man yet, to stay in such a vulnerable place. He talked Lewis into accompanying him back to the States.

So Lewis decided he had pushed his luck long enough, and he joined Colonel Russell's party of eighty-five men. When Lewis arrived at the safety of Russell's camp, he felt much elation and relief to be away from Fort Mann. His rash decision to stay there reflected on his immaturity, but as he learned from experience and gained in manhood, he made a better decision.

Early in camp one morning, the call of "Injuns" was heard. Lewis joined five others to ride out and reconnoiter. Determining that about four hundred Comanche braves were on the march toward them, they made haste back to the circling wagon train and readied for an attack. They had just finished making preparations when the braves charged. The dissonant and savage war whoops became more and more menacing as they charged and then withdrew, only to charge again. Lewis described the excitement of the battle as the warriors, riding on the sides of their horses for cover, circled the wagons time and time again, shooting from under their horse's necks.

After an hour, to the relief of the wagon train, the Indians withdrew. Lewis felt that had they not gotten their wagons circled in time and been able to set up good defensive positions, they would all have been scalped. He finally had gotten a taste of Indian fighting that he thought he would get at Fort Mann.

During the following day, the Comanches made their presence known, and they appeared to be looking for an opportunity to attack. Lewis was part of a small group that rode ahead to find a suitable camping spot. The group was made up of three riders on mules, including Lewis, and three on horses.

Lewis was off his mule, gathering wood, when the three horsemen suddenly, without a word, took off for the wagons. He looked up and saw a war party of about forty braves dashing out to try to cut him and the other two riders off from the wagon train. As Lewis and Colonel Russell dashed for the wagons that were now also under attack, the third member of their party was falling behind on his poor mule. About three hundred yards from the wagons, Lewis looked back and saw that

Coolidge wouldn't make it. He called to the Colonel, and they pulled up and shot the braves who were almost upon poor Coolidge.

There was no time for congratulations as Lewis and Coolidge made it into the wagon circle, but Lewis had saved a life by his cool determination to help. The Indians charged and withdrew for a couple of hours before giving up in the face of the strong defense put up from the wagons. It was a scary day for Lewis, but he had gotten more experience of an Indian fight. He couldn't help but admire the graceful Indian riders and their beautiful horses.

Once the caravan was out of Indian territory, Lewis joined Colonel Russell and a small party that left the wagon train to make a hard ride to reach civilization. They hoped to cover two hundred miles in three days to reach the first frontier town, Westport. Their first night in town, they sat down to a meal at a table with plates and utensils, only to laugh at themselves when they forgot their manners and fell back into the habit of eating with fingers and a scalp knife. Lewis promptly shopped for "civilized garments" at the store of a nephew of Daniel Boone's. He reluctantly gave away his old blue blanket that had been his house and pillow for so long.

Lewis separated from his companions and traveled to Fort Leavenworth to get his pay for the services he had provided to the army at Fort Mann. Then he traveled by steamboat to family and friends.

Thus ends the incredible story of a seventeen-year old-boy on the Santa Fe Trail. Lewis traveled for adventure and fun. He learned an amazing amount, living among men who knew how to survive on their own. And he learned from the Indians with whom he camped. He had learned to admire and respect them. It would be hard to imagine a way for a boy of seventeen today to have such adventures and to learn so much about self-reliance.

It is very fortunate that Lewis was also a prolific writer of his experiences, thoughts, and feelings. His journals are a superb record of many aspects of life on the Santa Fe Trail and beyond. What a privilege for us to see this adventure through the eyes of a very young man with courage, curiosity, acute observation, compassion, and enthusiasm. The Santa Fe Trail was for Lewis a passage to manhood.

8

MARION SLOAN RUSSELL
ON THE TRAIL TO WESTERN SETTLEMENT

THE MEMOIRS OF MARION* Sloan Russell are among the most touching of the records of travel on the Santa Fe Trail. For Marion, the trail not only led to a lifelong love of freedom but also to the experiences of a frontierswoman, which took her through years of joys and sorrows. The scope of her reminiscences covers from the time she first traveled the trail, at the age of seven, until she was in her eighties, when she dictated her memories of five round-trip passages on the Santa Fe Trail and her experiences as a settler. Her schoolteacher daughter-in-law, Mrs. Hal Russell, faithfully recorded the warm, sensitive recollections of her aging mother-in-law in *Land of Enchantment*, which related the excitement and adventure of the young traveler.

---

* I have used the name spelling as it was engraved on her tombstone and in surviving family papers, as M-a-r-i-o-n (with an "o"). Her daughter-in-law, Mrs. Hal Russell, changed the spelling, for no known reason, to M-a-r-i-a-n (with an "a"), in her book *Land of Enchantment*. Of interest is that Marion was listed as a male on the 1850 census record.

Marion's love of the land grew out of her early experiences of travel across the prairies. Her record of life as a settler has provided us with a unique and intelligent picture of how the settlement of the West unfolded for individual lives. The western pioneers were diverse, from many nations. They were men and women of every race, color, and creed, who believed in democracy, freedom, law, and order. God was a very real presence for many of them. They dealt with Indian wars, range wars, land and mineral wars, vigilantes, outlaws, unexpected death, disease, hunger, thirst, and disastrous weather. The loss of many loved ones was probably the most heartbreaking cost. Marion personified the emotions, stresses, and reactions to both the happy experiences that she nurtured from her childhood through her adult life, and the tragedies of her later life.

Born in Peoria, Illinois, Marion was the third and last child of William and Eliza St. Clair Sloan. They were of Scottish ancestry. Marion was born on January 26, 1845. Though the first child born to her parents died in infancy, she and her brother William lived to maturity. Marion never knew her father. Her mother told her he died at Monterrey, Mexico, in the Mexican War. Her stepfather, whom she remembered and loved, was killed by Indians while working as a scout.

After her second husband's death, Eliza Sloan traveled with William and Marion to Kansas City, Missouri. Eliza waited there for two years for her father to come from California to take her and the children to live with him. After they found out that Grandfather Sloan and his two sons had died in a cholera epidemic in 1852, Eliza decided to travel to California with her children on her own. It was a bold decision for a woman with two children to make this trip unescorted by a man.

They went to Fort Leavenworth, situated in present-day Kansas, to join the wagon train of well-known wagon master Francis Xavier Aubry. Eliza had confidence in him and he befriended the children, always looking out for them. He served as a surrogate protector of the family. Almost daily, wagon trains left Fort Leavenworth on the rutted Santa Fe Trail. In 1852, commerce to New Mexico was thriving, despite the dangers.

On the day they left Fort Leavenworth, a cholera epidemic was raging through the fort. The authorities were burning tar barrels in the streets, believing that might help ward off the dreaded disease. As the caravan left, the travelers felt they were leaving one danger to face others, but they felt there was safety in numbers on the prairie, with more than five hundred wagons in the train. Captain Aubry's wagons were followed by government wagons with supplies for Fort Union in New Mexico. Fort Union was the military supply depot for the Southwest.

The heavily loaded wagons of military equipment and merchandise for trade took over two months to reach Fort Union. The caravan moved slowly, with the ever-present threats of Indian attack, storms, and constant shortages of water. Sometimes the buffalo herds were so huge that it seemed like they would overrun the wagons. Sudden changes in weather would cause them to hunker down in the wagons to endure thunder, lightning, deluges of water, and high winds. Marion's memories of those squalls were dominated by the beauty of the post-storm sunsets. She was an impressionable child, who held such reminiscences dear for a lifetime.

On a typical day of travel, Marion's mother sat high on the wagon seat with her sun bonnet on, for she sun burned easily. She would knit or peel potatoes to keep busy. Eliza earned their passage by cooking for some of the wagon train members. Brother Will would walk all day with Pierre, the driver. Will grew suntanned and hardy. His job was to build cook fires for their mother. As soon as his job was completed, Will would scamper off to spend time with Captain Aubry. Both Marion and Will adapted quickly and loved the travel. It was a relatively unfettered time for their rambunctious and curious personalities, though they dared not wander far from the train.

At seven, Marion was too small to keep up walking, so she sat with her mother and played with her dolls or crawled back into the wagon to rest on their pile of bedding. Sitting on the hard, jolting wooden seat all day was pretty uncomfortable. A slow mule-drawn wagon would not provide a lot in the way of scenery change for entertainment.

As she related her experience in her old age, many scenes of the old trail remained vivid for her. She regretted that after the railroads came, the trail faded as grass grew over it. She felt that it continued to live only in the hearts of a few old people who could remember it. She could still recall the weary drivers sleeping under the wagons during their noon stop. She remembered the tired, sweaty mules rolling in the grass, so delighted to be free of their heavy harness. Babies were born on the trail and death took others away to unmarked graves.

She spoke about a Catholic Sister on her way to Santa Fe to serve in the school, who died of fright from the Indians. The nun was buried in a wagon rut, and the wagons passed over her grave to obliterate any sign of the grave, to protect it from wolves and Indians. Marion felt the Sister rested now without fear, while holding her crucifix.

At night, Captain Aubry's wagons circled, with a no-man's land between them and the government supply wagons. The children played in the area between the trains, where everyone could keep an eye on them. Mothers lived with a constant fear of an Indian snatching a child. The youngsters played ball, leapfrog, and "dare base" in this playground. One night, Marion lingered as it grew dark. As both wagon trains lit fires and the sound of voices and laughter came to her, the night seemed magical. Soon her worried mother was calling for her. It was dangerous to dawdle in the dark.

One dark night at Pawnee Rock, in what is now Kansas, they were awakened by whooping Indians. All was confusion within the circle of wagons, because the mules were frightened of Indians and they were running and braying in panic. Marion and her family had to get in the wagon when their tent collapsed during the fracas.

In the morning, the government herd of two hundred horses was gone. Captain Aubry would not proceed to Bent's Fort without the horses for the army. They had to wait for two weeks while riders went back to Fort Leavenworth to get another herd.

Every day they were visited by threatening Indians, but the wagon train was so large that the Indians never attacked. Captain Aubry warned the children daily to be on the alert and not wander off. He cautioned them that the Indians would steal the hair from their heads if they weren't careful. For Marion, that fear made her heedful and aware, but it did not limit her enjoyment. She was not the shrinking-violet type.

When the wagon train traveled the Cimarron Route, a shortcut across a very dry section of trail, Marion's job was to gather buffalo chips for fires. She would carefully kick each one over before picking it up, because there were often large spiders, centipedes, or scorpions underneath. She also became acquainted with big, hairy tarantulas, little lizards, and birds called roadrunners. Marion found childish delight in the nature around her. And she learned from one of Captain Aubry's tales that the muddy water in the buffalo wallows had been known to save the life of a wandering person dying of thirst. He said that gnats and impurities didn't stop a person who was that thirsty.

There was a two-day period when the wagon train had no water. As thirsty as Marion got, she felt sorrier for the tired mules than for herself. She, her mother Eliza, and Will had to wash in the same basin of water. Eliza determined that Will should wash last because he was the dirtiest.

Due to the layover at Pawnee Rock, they were late arriving at Fort Union. Snow had begun to fly, and it was cold. Sighting the fort provided great relief. It had been built the year before, in 1851, so the government could try to protect travelers from hostile Indians. It served as headquarters for the Ninth Military Department and the supply depot for the entire Southwestern region. It was also the base for troops during the long period of Americanization of the Territory of New Mexico, after it came under the authority of the United States as a result of the Mexican War.

At Fort Union, the caravan rested. The mules were turned out to forage for grass on the prairie. The two hundred horses were turned over to the military. Officers came and sat on the fence to watch the horses and choose their mounts. Soldiers were very busy unloading the freight. Marion's camp was outside the gate, and she and Will could roam freely all day, watching the exciting action. Nevertheless, children traveling the trail learned to live and survive with a lot of fear and brutality that most children in the United States don't have to deal with today. One night, Indians attacked the stage area that was two miles from the fort. Eliza had the children dress quickly, and they went inside the stockade to stand in the cold and wait. They could see the burning station in the distance and hear the blood-curdling war whoops of the Indians. It was a very scary night. The next day, returning troops reported that one of the men who tended the stock was scalped, and all the horses were stolen. There is no explanation for why the troops didn't rush out over the short distance and try to help the men.

When the mules were rested, on a cold December morning, the wagon train was ready to proceed to Santa Fe to deliver its freight. The family was very excited to see Santa Fe, thinking it would be a city like they saw in the East. However, they were in Santa Fe before they realized it, and what they saw was not what they expected. They crossed a water ditch, where half-naked children watched them with curiosity. They passed through a wooden gateway that arched over them. Among low, square adobe houses, they rode along alley-like streets crowded with Mexicans, Indians, and people of mixed race. Donkeys, goats, and chickens wandered everywhere. Marion's mother kept her children in the wagon until the mules were unharnessed and led away. The bedlam was too great for them to be allowed off the wagon and into the chaos.

At this point in telling her story, Marion recalled that two years later, Captain Aubry would be killed in an argument. She remembered him as a brave man and a great leader, who guided huge wagon trains across the prairies. She related how, on a bet, he rode from Santa Fe to Independence, Missouri, in under six days. He made it, but upon arrival he fell from his horse with exhaustion. He was one of several Western heroes she would admire and know as a friend.

Leaving Santa Fe, the Sloan family continued their long journey in anticipation of traveling on to Sutter's Fort in the gold fields of California. However, another outcome lay in store for them. One night, on the way to Albuquerque, a young Mexican boy was lingering around their camp. He stole the basket that contained the jewels and money with which Eliza was financing the trip. This was a disaster, and new plans had to be formulated.

In Albuquerque, Eliza left the wagon train and rented a house. She began to make a living running a boarding house, once again proving her self-sufficiency. Most of the boarders were Indian scouts.

After living in Albuquerque for a couple of years, Marion's mother decided in the spring of 1854 to move to Santa Fe, where she felt they would be safer from crime. She rented a home and again opened it to lodgers, who were mostly military men who paid forty-five dollars a month for room and board.

Marion began formal education in a Santa Fe school established in 1852 by Bishop Lamy. He had convinced six Loretto nuns from a convent in Kentucky to travel the Santa Fe Trail to set up a school for girls in the predominantly illiterate capital. Tragically, one sister died of cholera in Independence and another had to turn back due to illness.

In the first year, their school enrolled one hundred girls; ninety-five were Mexican and five were American. Marion was one of the five. Ninety-nine of the girls were Catholic. The sisters lovingly called Marion their "little heretic." Marion loved many of the nuns and was always grateful for the education she got with them. Though she remained a non-believer, she always appreciated the devoted sisters and admired the work of Bishop Lamy. While living in Santa Fe, the Catholic Church was always a presence in their lives.

One evening as Marion returned from school, she met a man walking from the plaza. He smiled with gentle, kind eyes. He engaged her in conversation, and she exchanged a few shy words with him. Later she was to be more proud of her acquaintance with this man than of any other. The man was Colonel Kit Carson. Years later, when Marion had married a young soldier and was stationed at Fort Nichols, Colonel Carson was her husband's commanding officer and her trusted friend and mentor.

Marion recalled some of the history of the life of Kit Carson, but she knew him as a friend and knew his wife Josefa as well. Marion could see in his eyes the love that Kit felt for his "Little Jo." Kit was a lonely, shy man with a great heart. He related best with children and simple folk, like himself. She felt it was only natural for him to marry among the Mexicans—people he loved and protected. Marion's opinion reflects a prejudice of the time against whites marrying Mexicans or Indians. But she recognized that Kit had done both, and she understood that was what was right for him. She remembered him as an uncouth, awkward man who spoke in the Western vernacular, his use of the language revealing his illiteracy. She described this couple as a virile Indian scout and a beautiful, young girl. She esteemed Kit as a hero with human frailties.

Marion's mother did the family doctoring with homeopathic remedies, and she kept a very clean house, though the old adobe houses were infested with bed-bugs. Marion recalled how her mother would twice weekly carry their hand-carved wooden beds outdoors and pour boiling water over them to kill the bedbug eggs. She soon eliminated the pests, but she never let up in her battle against them. The beds also had to be draped with mosquito netting, for there were no screens on the windows.

In August 1856, Eliza took her family back across the Santa Fe Trail to Fort Leavenworth. The caravan had only twenty wagons, which offered little protection from Indians. They were drawn by oxen this time, which made for a slow trip, but the large animals provided more stability for reading and sewing in the wagons because of their plodding pace. Marion's family was able to sleep in the wagon, though some of the wagons were full of buffalo hides for Eastern markets. Marion was now eleven and Will was thirteen. He walked beside the wagon again.

Surprisingly, Marion could remember nothing remarkable about this trip. It was often boring and tiresome. The August heat was wilting for everyone. They had one Indian scare when her mother refused to give food to an Indian and he became threatening. However, the wagon master ran him off by brandishing a knife. The wagon master was uneasy about the situation, but they were able to proceed without further incident.

One day the caravan took an afternoon break from the heat under some trees, and the women took advantage of the rest to do some laundry. Because they had a full moon that night, they decided to travel on during the cooler hours. As the men walked by the wagons, riders dozed in their saddles, and the women and children slept in the wagons.

In the late hours, they were awakened by the war cries of Apaches. The oxen stampeded and scattered the wagons in every direction. The oxen ran until they were exhausted and the Indians had given up the chase. In the morning, the outriders brought all twenty wagons back to the trail. Fear rode with them after that, and they never knew why the Apaches had not massacred everyone.

Eighteen fifty-six was the first year of what Marion refers to as the "John Brown disturbance." John Brown was an abolitionist who set out to free the slaves. Additionally, as territories were considered for statehood, there were debates, often leading to violence, about whether any specific state should be slave or free. Along the trail, there were many burned-out homes and rumors of women and children being tortured and killed by opposing factions.

In Kansas, pro-slavery Border Ruffians from Missouri and anti-slavery Free-State advocates from Kansas were fighting over this issue, and the Border Ruffians were riding roughshod over everyone. When the small wagon train arrived at Diamond Spring, Kansas, the men decided to stay there until a larger train or some troops came along to provide more security from Indians and Ruffians. Eliza didn't think they were any safer in camp than on the trail, but, being a woman, she was not heeded.

After two weeks in camp, the food supplies began to run low. After another meeting, the men voted to continue staying in camp. Marion's mother announced that she was more afraid of famine than of a bunch of Border Ruffians. She said she would walk if there was no other way to proceed. After another day of waiting, she awakened Marion early in the morning and told her to dress quickly. They were going to walk to the next stop on the trail, Council Grove. She told Will to stay with their things to guard them.

As Marion and Eliza walked through the cold dawn, Marion wished she had been chosen to stay with the wagons. About a mile down the road, they met a rider on a mule. Eliza challenged him and asked if he was a Border Ruffian. He laughed and said he was no ruffian. When he heard the story of the wagons at Diamond Spring, he thought the cowardice of the men was very funny. He said he owned that property and he would throw them out. He told Eliza there were no Border Ruffians between them and Council Grove.

It was sixteen miles to Council Grove, but a very tired Marion and her mother made it. The kindly grocery store keeper gave them a bed for the night, and the next morning they were able to get a ride back to the wagons in the fancy buggy of a man traveling westward.

Marion decided that day that she wanted to spend her life traveling back and forth on the Santa Fe Trail. She loved the trail and the open, free existence. She thought those were the best days of her life. When they arrived at Fort Leavenworth, both Marion and Will felt deep regret that the trip was over. They had to resign themselves to the limits of civilization.

The spring of 1860 found Marion's family still at Fort Leavenworth. There was much talk that sounded like the first rumblings of civil war. Discussions were endless about the Fugitive Slave Act, the Missouri Compromise, the *Dred Scott* decision, and the John Brown raid. One morning, as Marion and Will were reminiscing about Santa Fe, their mother announced that she was as homesick for the West as they were. She would book them on the first train west that she could find. Marion and Will whooped. Marion was now fifteen and Will was seventeen.

They were able to obtain passage with a two hundred-wagon caravan. Because of their numbers and the government forts now built to protect travelers on the trail, they didn't feel as much fear of Indians as before.

As they headed west, Marion and Will remembered a woman they had met on their last trip east. They had encountered a house where there were several men and one pregnant, abused-looking woman. She approached them in a fearful manner, and Marion's mother had asked the wagon master to intervene on her behalf, but he wouldn't. One of the men from the house chased them away in a hostile manner, and they left the pitiful woman behind with much concern for her.

Now heading west again, Marion and Will wondered if they would see her and her baby. When they came to the house, it was deserted. Will found a grave half covered with weeds. A board marking the grave recorded the death of Sarah Grace Austin and her infant daughter, with a date from shortly after their earlier encounter. This was a poignant moment for Marion and Will. They wished they could have helped this battered woman and her unborn child.

Once in a while, a herd of wild horses would swoop down on them in a thunderous charge. These were wild animals, descendants of horses the Indians had stolen from the wagon trains or that had simply been lost or abandoned along the Santa Fe and Oregon Trails. Today there are still small herds of these descendants in a few pockets of wild land in the West, though they are fast being exterminated.

The Sloan's route west did not follow the Cimarron Route this time but followed the longer, easier route to

Bent's Fort and over the Raton Pass into New Mexico from Colorado. Some of the people headed north from Bent's Fort to follow gold fever to Pike's Peak, but many, including Marion and her family, continued on the route to Santa Fe.

Raton Pass was still the steep and tortuous climb that it had always been. By midday, the horses were jaded and six of the wagons had broken axles. When they finally traversed the pass and arrived at Fort Union, they found that the troops there had accomplished their task of making that part of the frontier much safer from Indian attack. Attacks by the Indians in northern New Mexico had become rather rare during that period (though they would later increase again).

Marion was delighted to arrive back in Santa Fe that autumn of 1860. She soon shed whatever Eastern ways she had acquired and settled down into her school uniform and the school routine. Her mother returned to the same house and had more boarders than she could handle. They loved eating again with hot chili seasoning, and they visited with their neighbors in the now comfortable native tongue, Spanish.

After a year, Marion's mother decided to return to Fort Leavenworth. Marion never knew what motivated her mother to go back, but she thought it was the lure of the trail. At heart, her mother was a nomad, and she happily traveled back and forth on the trail for one reason, then another. So once more, they departed on mule-drawn wagons.

Only a year had passed, but Marion noticed many changes along the trail. Here and there they came across the house of a settler and bits of plowed land. The Indians were there, but so were the white men. The Indians were losing the fight for the land. On the plains, white men were killing the buffalo in great numbers, while the Indians watched sullenly as their great herds were being destroyed.

They returned this time to Kansas City, and Marion went back to school, while Will went to work on the newspaper and studied for the ministry. When the Civil War started, Will joined a Kansas regiment and marched away to war. Marion and her mother put up a brave front when it was time for Will to leave. They maintained a façade of smiles despite their terrible fears for him. Marion recalled that, had they known that they would not see Will again for fifty years, they would not have been so brave.

After the war, Will was ordained as a Baptist minister, sent as a missionary to India, and then assigned as a minister to Mexico City. Surprisingly, when he returned to the United States, he renounced the Baptist Church and joined the Catholic Church. Marion never heard him say why he did that, but she believed that the early seeds of Catholicism planted by Father Lamy, long ago in Santa Fe, had born fruit.

In the spring of 1862, Marion's mother was scheduled to travel the trail again to Santa Fe. Marion was to stay behind and marry in Kansas City. Her mother had told her that her desire to return West would be delayed until she knew Marion was safely married. However, at the last moment, Marion broke off her engagement and headed West once again with her mother. This would be their fifth trip over the trail. Marion said that the lure of the trail still held them. This was the last trip over the trail for Marion, but not for her mother. Eventually her mother made it to California and lived out a prosperous life. She was buried near the waters of the Pacific Ocean.

In 1864, Marion met Lieutenant Richard D. Russell. It was love at first sight. Six months later, in February 1865, they were married at Fort Union. Marion was twenty, and her mother had sent to Kansas City for her lovely trousseau. After their wedding, they were stationed at Fort Union for a while, and they lived in quarters next door to Colonel Kit Carson.

*Lt. Richard and Marion Russell
(PD-US)*

As Marion looked back in her memoirs, she remembered how her own life story and the story of the fort were strangely interwoven. Union Fort was the first

*Some of the preserved ruins at Fort Union, New Mexico,
showing the hospital (Fort Union National Monument)*

refuge she encountered on her initial trip west. On each trip across the trail, it continued providing a place of safety. She eventually met the man she loved while there. She also lived there as a young wife and made friends with Kit Carson, when she and her husband served at the fort. It always had a warm place in her heart for many happy memories.

The government was constructing a string of forts further out along the Santa Fe Trail, to protect travelers from increasingly hostile Indians. When Lt. Russell was ordered to go to Fort Nichols under Colonel Carson, Marion wanted to go along. Colonel Carson told her it wasn't safe for her to go, and he had promised her mother to keep her secure. He said he would send for her as soon as it was safe, and he did. Marion revered Kit as a friend and protector.

In September 1865, they received orders from Colonel Carson to abandon Fort Nichols and return to Fort Union for reassignment. It was quite an emotional scene for Marion when the troops formed up, the bugles sounded, the wagons rolled, and the sounds of all the movement heralded the departure. The flag was left flying, and posted on the flagpole was a warning to anyone against destroying government property.

Marion had a happy life with Richard. When he left the military, they ran a trading post for a while in Tecolate, between Fort Union and Santa Fe. After their business partner absconded with their profits, they moved to southern Colorado and pioneered a remote valley. They raised a family, worked hard, prospered, and watched their valley being settled by other families. Marion seemed to thrive on all that it took to be a pioneer woman.

In 1888, they received notice that they were living on land belonging to the Maxwell Land Grant, an old

Spanish grant. They were given twenty-four hours to abandon the domain they had wrestled from the wilderness. Richard worked to represent the interests of the people who had settled in the Stonewall Valley. While carrying a flag of truce to negotiate, Richard was shot by deputies hired by the Maxwell Company. He lay suffering for five days before he died. There were other men killed, and a terrible injustice was perpetrated on the people who had worked so hard to build homes and a community on land that appeared to be there for the settling. Marion felt that the bullet that killed Richard also killed her, but there were children to care for, and she had to go on.

As Marion was relating her memories to her daughter-in-law, six of her nine children were still living. She had sixteen grandchildren and twenty-two great-grandchildren. Marion Sloan Russell was symbolic of the strong, enduring pioneer woman.

When Marion was eighty-nine, she revisited sights on the Santa Fe Trail. Fort Nichols was overgrown. With her feet she traced the grass-filled wheel ruts where the wagon trains had gone creaking past. At Fort Union, she saw crumbling walls and tottering chimneys, but in her mind she could still hear a preacher say, "That which God hath joined together let no man put asunder." She could see and hear Colonel Carson assure her of his promise to her mother to keep her safe and watch over her. The wind moaned through the ruins and carried the sound of marching feet. She saw a child in a blue pinafore, sitting on a wagon seat. It was little "Maid Marion."

She found Santa Fe was a very changed city, too. The wooden gateway through which they had entered the city was gone. The plaza was neat and clean. She saw a woman in red slacks sitting in the very spot where she had watched Captain Aubry sit and read the newspaper. It was strange to stand that evening in the ruins of Fort Marcy. Was it her imagination that she could hear the voices of children playing there, eighty years before?

Marion tells us that her heart had grown tired. In her awareness of her fatigue with life, her heart returned to the land the old trail ran through. "I stand listening for the sound of wheels that never come; stand waiting for the clasp of arms long crumbled into dust."†

The Santa Fe Trail was in Marion's blood, thanks to her mother's nomadic ways and Marion's love of the freedom, beauty, and adventure she was blessed to know since childhood. The Santa Fe Trail had a profound effect on the life of this strong and sensitive woman. Thank goodness she shared her memories with us.

Marion Sloan Russell died on Christmas Day, 1936, from injuries resulting from an automobile accident. Ironically, after surviving all the dangers of pioneering in a wild land, she died from the technology of a machine, known as the "horseless carriage." She was buried next to Richard at a site she had chosen in 1876, because it was the "wildest and most beautiful place around."

An interesting side note about the lives of Marion and Eliza remains a mystery. Marion's father, William James Sloan, was an Army Surgeon. She had no memory of him, and her mother told her that he was killed at Monterrey, Mexico, during the Mexican War. Yet records show that Marion's father was alive until 1880. Eliza was

---

†   Marion Sloan Russell, *Land of Enchantment*, as dictated to Mrs. Hal Russell (Evanston, Illinois, The Branding Iron Press, 1954, and reprinted Albuquerque, University of New Mexico Press, 1981), 143.

most likely separated from Dr. William Sloan. Similarly, when Eliza married Jeremiah Mahoney, a soldier and Indian scout, she told Marion that Mr. Mahoney was killed by Indians when Marion was about five years old. Yet records show that Mr. Mahoney lived until 1899.

It is a mystery why Eliza told her children that these men were dead. Some of her travels in and out of Santa Fe and Fort Union may have had to do with Army Surgeon William James Sloan being assigned to the post of Chief Medical Officer of the Department of New Mexico in August 1856. Some of Eliza's travels may have been to keep her children away from where their father was serving. That would indicate that she had some information about her husband's location. He also remarried.

Maybe someday a record will be found to explain more about their situation. Something like a long-lost letter might give us more information on this mystery. Part of the fun of being a historian is the detective work involved.

9

JAMES ROSS LARKIN

ON THE TRAIL TO HEALTH

In September 1856, James Larkin traveled the Santa Fe Trail for health reasons. James was among the vanguard of "health seekers" to travel West for the restorative powers of the clear air. By the 1880s, the idea of gentlemen health seekers journeying West would lead to health resorts cropping up in places like Colorado Springs, Colorado.

James was born July 31, 1831, in Wilmington, Delaware. When he was six years old, his parents moved to St. Louis, Missouri, a booming commercial center. James's father was a very successful merchant, and the family prospered.

Sickness was very common in the Mississippi Valley during the nineteenth century. Malaria, dysentery, tuberculosis, yellow fever, cholera, diphtheria, pneumonia, and small pox sent many people to early graves. Cold, damp weather, and poor housing made everyone vulnerable. Because doctors could only treat symptoms of these diseases, they often suggested travel into the drier climate of the Southwest. James's poor health eventually led to the decision to follow this advice, after he had tried the mountains of Virginia for the same reason. Our knowledge of exactly what was wrong is speculative, but it is believed he suffered from chronic dyspepsia, a common ailment of the time that is difficult to define. It was probably inflammation of the stomach or intestine. He also had frequent bouts of neuralgia— another nineteenth-century catch-all word for problems due to the aftereffects of malaria.

James wrote that he returned home from the Catskill Mountains and other points in the East, where he was seeking a cure. Since his health had not improved, his mother and friends urged him to travel west on the Santa Fe Trail. They placed their hopes in the doctors' theory that a curative trip on the plains might help. Accordingly, James contacted the successful trader and frontiersman William Bent, of the family that established Bent's trading fort in Colorado. Bent welcomed James to join a wagon train going to the fort in September 1856.

James would keep a diary of his journey that was unique in a couple of ways. He was known as a health-seeker, and he brought that different perspective to his travels. He also provided a distinctive insight to his travels on the trail and to the character of the well-known pioneer William Bent.

James had to make hasty preparations because Bent planned to leave St. Louis the next day. James could catch up at the jumping-off point of Westport, where Bent would spend several days preparing the wagon train.

Because of the financial backing of his family, James was able to cross the Santa Fe Trail in comfort. He purchased a costly wagon, harness, saddle, a pair of mules, a horse, and piles of assorted gear. He would travel in a relatively luxurious style, much like Susan Magoffin (see Chapter 6). With assistance from his cousin, who was a local merchant, James made arrangements and set off by train and steamboat for Westport. Travel was not easy, and missed connections happened back then too. There was a delay in the arrival of the steamboat, so James set off a little late for Westport, with his new carriage and all his freight. His list of supplies included things like a buffalo robe, a heavy coat, a pillowcase, supplies to make bullets, cooking gear, opera glasses, and letters of introduction. The list was very extensive.

When arriving in Kansas City, Missouri, James went right out to Westport, despite rumors of ruffians in the area. He saw drunken characters who he thought should probably be hanged, but local people did not seem concerned. From his writing, one senses that James was a sheltered young man who was taken aback by some of the rough people he was encountering. This trip was going to expose his delicate side to new, sometimes crude, experiences. He entertained second thoughts about his journey, until he met Mr. Bent, who seemed relaxed and assured. James's apprehensions were relieved.

James kept a very detailed account of his expenses on the trip, reflecting his background in a successful family of businessmen. He bought a pair of mules for $325 and a small horse for $100. On Mr. Bent's recommendation, James hired Jim Young to drive his carriage, to care for his mules and horse, and in general to be useful. Young was paid $25 a month. James was pleased that Mr. Young started right away by cooking a good meal.

On September 25, 1856, James started with William Bent's wagons. They traveled slowly, to work out any kinks in their equipment and animals. It was a chance to see that everything was working correctly and to fix any problems. James camped for the first time at Indian Creek, after this laborious shakedown. On the morning of the 27th, James's horse was missing. His tracks led in the direction of Westport. Early in a trip, it was common for the livestock to try to return home. An Indian was dispatched to bring the horse back, and the caravan went on.

The next day, they covered about twenty miles and camped near what is today Lawrence, Kansas. They were still seeing houses along the trail, but many were burned, and one was even still smoldering. They were seeing the results of the fight going on over slavery in new states. As Kansas was approaching acceptance into statehood, both pro-slavery Border Ruffians from Missouri and Free-State advocates in Kansas fought brutally to try to determine whether Kansas would be a state where slavery was legal or not. This lawlessness caused apprehension among the travelers, but James's party encountered no trouble.

James expressed pleasure with the food so far, as they got some local fresh watermelons and milk. He was able to write about his lost horse to his mother and others back in St. Louis, via mail that passed between Council Grove and Westport. He borrowed a horse to ride, but it was very cold for the time of year. He found riding a horse warmer than being in the carriage, probably due to the horse's body heat.

As usual on the trail, James found many nations represented among the people traveling and working. Americans, Mexicans, French, German, and Pawnees made up the sixteen men of their group. He mentioned that Mr. Bent's Cheyenne wife, Owl Woman, and a Pawnee Indian boy were with the train. The boy had been a prisoner but was purchased by Mr. Bent, and Owl Woman was very fond of the boy. Here are examples of two customs of the West that were questioned by Easterners. Marrying an Indian was considered immoral, as was buying a person, at least outside of the slave-holding South. However, mores outside the borders of "civilization" were very different and often rooted in practicality. It was not at all uncommon for mountain men, like Bent, to marry Indian women.

On October 3, riders from Bent's Fort informed William Bent of some problem at the fort that James did not elaborate on. When Bent decided to ride ahead to get to the fort more quickly, James chose to ride with him. With two carriages and a provision wagon, they started that night and rode hard. Their hope was to reach the fort in seven to eight days. When they saw a large herd of buffalo, Bent did take time to shoot several, and they were delighted with the fresh meat. Interestingly, William Bent was not concerned with traveling for a week or so with such a small group. His years as a trader and mountain man apparently allowed him to have confidence in his ability to get the small group to the fort without being attacked by Indians.

They reached Cow Creek on a day that was eighty-nine degrees, and James took advantage of the stream to bathe. There was very little opportunity for such a luxury. When they reached Walnut Creek, there was a small trading post. A rough set of men were hanging around the post and seemed to be entertaining designs on the four mules pulling the provision wagon. Luckily, though they no doubt wanted to steal the mules, there was no trouble.

When they heard there was a camp of Cheyenne Indians nearby, Bent sent a message that he would like to talk to them. The Indians soon galloped into camp and enjoyed a feast of bread and coffee while talking with Bent. They were young warriors on the warpath against some Pawnees. William Bent's connection with the Cheyennes, through his wife, Owl Woman, provided much security. They were able to socialize with these enthusiastic young men, despite their fierce appearance. James felt that with any other leader of their small group, they would have been in trouble. Maybe this relationship with the Cheyennes was the main reason Bent felt comfortable rushing ahead of the wagon train in a small group. On this occasion and the next day, when again running into some Cheyenne warriors, James found them very ferocious looking. He commented that they were very well dressed, but their horses looked very poor.

On the 13th, they reached Bent's Fort on the north side of the Arkansas River. Here Bent traded with Cheyenne, Kiowa, Arapaho, and Comanche Indians. The Indians brought in antelope and dear skins, buffalo

Bent's Fort in southeastern Colorado
(Bent's Old Fort National Historic Site)

robes, and dried buffalo meat to trade for coffee, sugar, flour, gunpowder, and rifle balls. Sugar was a favorite extravagance of the Indians, who ate it raw. The measure of trade was how many robes a thing was worth.

Upon arrival at the fort, James learned that the trouble had been between Indians and troops farther north. The Cheyennes, Arapahos, and Comanches were friendly with Bent, the Kiowas a little less so. However, some Cheyennes had been killed near Fort Laramie (in what is now Wyoming), so those Cheyennes had gone on the warpath and killed some whites. It was safe at the fort, though, because of Bent's friendship with the local Indians, so James did not feel much apprehension about this outbreak farther north.

James felt homesick and gloomy when he reached the fort. He didn't like the state of affairs, the lifestyle, or the condition of society. This was a crude, rough place and not what he expected. He tried to keep in good humor, but he felt his health wasn't any better than it had been in the mountains of Virginia, where he could have stayed for less expense.

For this wealthy young man who had enjoyed the variety and interest of the trail, life at the fort just didn't measure up. He found the diet of dried buffalo meat boiled with corn, coffee, sugar, biscuits, and butter rather monotonous. He also thought that the manner in which the men lived with the Indian women rather loose—very different than in "civilization." James was a privileged traveler who was not as enamored with wilderness life as were most of our young travelers.

James's amusements were few. One day, he showed Bent how to work a spinning top Bent had brought to sell to the Indian children. The trader had also brought out jumping jacks. A toy that cost ten cents in the States would be traded for a buffalo robe worth seven dollars in St. Louis. James felt Bent was turning a pretty good profit. James also had been entertained by performing well in a shooting match and buying a nice horse from Bent. But he was soon bored. Late in October, when an opportunity came to leave with some supply wagons going to Moro, New Mexico, he was glad to join them. Indian troubles around the fort had been making him uneasy by now. He felt this was a good opportunity to progress toward Santa Fe with safety.

After a difficult passage over Raton Pass, they traveled into New Mexico. Near Rayado, they met Kit Carson with some men going out on a hunt. James doesn't elaborate on that meeting, but he certainly knew of the famous frontiersman.

James's party spent a night enjoying the hospitality of Mr. Lucien Maxwell, owner of a vast property, where he ran thousands of head of cattle. Lucien Maxwell had married a wealthy Mexican woman and, thereby, became the owner of the Maxwell Land Grant. Maxwell extended generous hospitality to travelers through the area. James commented on their wonderful breakfast of venison, eggs, cheese, and molasses.

On November 7, after a long day of traveling forty-two miles, the tired mules brought them to Moro, a poor Mexican village of adobe houses located north of Las Vegas, New Mexico. While there, James attended a fandango similar to those that many Americans attended in Santa Fe. He felt the dancers were very graceful. The music was provided by fiddles and a guitar. Everyone smoked all the time, there was a barroom attached to the dance hall, and a woman sat among those at the gambling table. Americans visiting New Mexico in this period often felt the morals of the people were very loose.

Gambling, much dancing, and certainly smoking and drinking were frowned upon, especially for women, in the United States of the time. James reported this behavior without commenting on how he felt about it, though one senses disapproval.

On November 12, James left Moro to proceed to Santa Fe. The caravan leader, a merchant named Mr. William A. Bransford, was traveling with four little girls going to the convent in Santa Fe. James commented that they could be called "half-breeds," because their mothers were Mexican, thus expressing a prejudice of the time against white men marrying Mexican women. Two of the little girls traveled with James in his carriage. He found them quite annoying.

In three days, they arrived in Santa Fe and left the little girls at the convent. Then they went to the Fonda Hotel for accommodations. It was a gathering place for gentlemen. James found the "table" very excellent and the hotel well kept. However, he felt that $2.50 per day for food and lodging, plus $1.00 to feed his horse, was costly.

On Sundays, the stores stayed open and James wondered at the Mexican women who believed that church attendance was mandatory, but then they went shopping. Where he came from in the East, keeping the Sabbath holy meant doing nothing on Sunday except worshipping and reading the Bible. This was a common reaction among Americans visiting this exotic culture. Again, he commented that the women had loose morals and the men were addicted to gambling and stealing.

On November 28, James traveled with Major Albert Smith, paymaster of the US Army, to take the troops' payroll to Albuquerque. Surprisingly, he wrote about attending church on the same day that he went to a fandango. Apparently, comments on the loose morals of the Mexicans didn't keep him from enjoying a busy Sunday with some entertainment. On December 1, they started back to Santa Fe, spending one night on the trip because the roads were so bad with snow. James was surprised at the severity of the winters in New Mexico.

Interestingly, in Santa Fe, James mentioned socializing regularly with Dr. and Mrs. Sloan. This is the Dr. Sloan who was the father of Marion Sloan Russell (see Chapter 8). Marion believed her father to have been dead since before she had any memory of him. Yet in December 1856, Dr. Sloan was living in Santa Fe. He had arrived in August of that year, having been appointed Chief Medical Officer of the Department of New Mexico. It also was in August that Marion's mother suddenly announced that she was concerned about her rented house back East falling into disrepair, and she departed Santa Fe with her two children. We can only speculate whether Eliza Sloan's sudden decision was related to knowing that the children's father was nearby.

Many times, the characters on the Santa Fe Trail had such close associations and intersecting story lines. By reading their different accounts, we get a fuller picture of their times. Another example of this is when James had an opportunity to visit Bishop Lamy at his ranch, about three miles out of town. James wrote that it was a romantic and beautiful spot, surrounded by mountains. When Marion Sloan Russell was a little girl attending Catholic school in Santa Fe, she wrote that the nuns said Bishop Lamy went to his ranch to refresh himself from time to time.

Though he was very busy socializing, especially visiting several of the leading ladies of the town during calling hours each day, James seemed to be getting restless and bored. He was often unwell with digestive problems, and he continued to feel he was not getting any better in New Mexico. In December, he consulted with Dr. Sloan about returning to the States by traveling to San Antonio, Texas. Dr. Sloan told him it would probably be as good for him as staying in Santa Fe.

Before James finalized his preparations to depart, his plans once again changed. He was offered a job as a clerk to Major Smith. Since the pay was good and the work was light, James accepted. He postponed his return to the States until the spring. New Year's Eve found James traveling to Fort Union with Major Smith to pay the troops there.

Spending the last evening of 1856 out in the wilderness, James wondered at how different things were than what he had anticipated on New Year's Eve the year before. He was far from the comforts of city life, but he marveled at all his experiences throughout the year. This passage in his journal speaks to all of us: we never know where the future will take us.

James arrived at Fort Union on January 2, commenting that he found the whitewashed homes of the fort much more attractive than the mud houses of Santa Fe. He helped complete the disbursement of the payroll, a sum of nearly $10,000, and then he returned to Santa Fe through the mountains and deep snow. James suffered from the cold in the carriage and was very glad to arrive back at the hospitable Fonda Hotel.

The next day, James observed a funeral procession for a child of about three years. The body was exposed in an open bier carried by four laughing, talking women. A boy carrying a cross preceded the procession, and a man playing lively tunes on a violin followed the bier. James was amazed at the lack of solemnity and mourning. He did not understand the belief of the people that the child was in a happier place and that there wasn't a need to be sad. Such stark cultural differences between the Mexicans and Americans were not understood by many people until they lived in New Mexico for a long time.

Abruptly at the end of January 1857, James's diary ended. He entered a meticulous final accounting of his expenses. He was apparently preparing to return to the States, but something happened to delay his departure until March 1857. It is known that he traveled the trail again at least one more time that same year and planned another trip in 1866, though it is not known whether he actually made that trip.

Though James often comes across as critical of much of what he sees, maybe he was just someone who expected a lot from himself and others. We will probably never learn what drew him back to travel on the trail again. Maybe it did benefit his health. We don't know how fully recovered his health was by being on the prairies, but he wasn't harmed by it, and his return to the West might indicate that he felt it was good for him. Due to the high altitude and dry air, travel on the trail may have been more beneficial for people with pulmonary health problems than for people with digestive issues.

James's health was never very robust. In 1859, after his return to St. Louis, he married. Over the years, he had eight children, of which six lived to maturity. He lived comfortably. Unfortunately, at age 43, he died of pneumonia on January 24, 1875.

James's great-grandson, Phillip D. Beall Jr., donated James's diary to the National Park Service in 1984. Barton H. Barbour was working at Bent's Old Fort National Historic Site, cataloging items on display when he found James's diary and recognized the value of it. He requested and received permission from the Park Service to transcribe, edit, and publish the diary for a wider readership. This is the type of discovery that really makes the day of a historian/detective.

10

WILLIAM B. NAPTON
ON THE TRAIL TO THE HUNT

FORTY YEARS AFTER THE fact, William B. Napton told the story of crossing the plains when he was eighteen years old, in *Over the Santa Fe Trail, 1857*. He referred to his health as "indifferent," and his doctor thought the trip might benefit him. He saw himself as an expert with gun and pistol and felt that he would "gratify" his sporting appetites by killing buffalo and elk. As a teenager with relatively little experience, he could not have dreamed of the adventures awaiting him.

So in April 1857, he set out to join a wagon train led by a state senator's son, who was twenty-five years old. "Jim Crow" Chiles was known to have killed several men, but William found him to be a considerate friend, usually good natured, but also subject to fits of anger.

Young Jim Crow had the skills to lead a wagon train, and by the first of May, the oxen and wagons had been gathered near the jumping off point, three miles from Westport, Missouri. William was impressed by the huge freight wagons built by Hiram Young, a free Negro of nearby Independence, which could hold seven or eight thousand pounds of merchandise. He noted that two wagons were full of imported champagne for Ceran St. Vrain, to be delivered to Las Vegas and Mora, in New Mexico, and he was impressed that such luxuries were enjoyed so far beyond the Missouri frontier.

There was a shortage of drivers, so when three men approached Captain Chiles looking for jobs one evening, he had to consider them. They were well dressed, with silk hats, and did not look at all like drivers. Though they admitted to knowing nothing about driving oxen, they were stranded and needed employment. Twenty-five dollars a month and board sounded good to them. Two of the men passed their probation and made decent workers, but the third, henceforth known as Skeesicks, was accomplished in penmanship and accounting and little else. He became an object of derision among the men. Much like Tete Rouge (see Chapter 5, Francis Parkman) Skeesicks was more of a detriment to the wagon train than an asset.

Among the teamsters was a young Mexican boy who would serve as interpreter with the Indians. Many of the Indians could speak Spanish but no English. There were men from Tennessee, Kentucky, Arkansas, and Texas. William also got acquainted with some of the Mexicans from nearby merchant trains that had arrived from Mexico. He noted that they subsisted on flour and dried buffalo meat. The supplies provided for William's merchant train were much more sumptuous, with bacon, flour, coffee, sugar, beans, and pickles.

William commented on the derivation of many of the Spanish and Mexican words used by the traders. It seemed to him that many pure Castilian words from Spain had undergone changes by the uneducated Mexicans. After the words had been "Mexicanized," they were further "Missourianized." *Cavayard*–a term used to refer to the guards of the horse herd — was thought to be a corruption of the Spanish word for horse attendant.

In Westport, William purchased a first-rate buffalo horse. It had come across the plains from California the previous year and proven to be very fast and fearless. He ran so close to a buffalo that William could almost touch the target. William, with his dreams of big-game hunting, was delighted to acquire this enhancement to his hunting skills.

On the tenth of June, 1857, they departed on their long journey. The weather was good, the government had laid out a straight road that could be traveled with ease, and everyone was in high spirits.

When they reached Turkey Creek, in Kansas, they were first able to spot a herd of buffalo. The great mass of shaggy beasts spread out over the prairie for several miles in all directions. The enthusiastic hunters rode quietly toward the herd until they were within several hundred yards, and then they charged. The group they pursued was a band of old bulls. William was so excited that he started shooting at a large one, knocking off tufts of hair but otherwise having little effect. After a run of a mile or two, the bull stopped and swung around to face William. William discharged his last remaining bullets, delivering what he thought were mortal wounds. After several minutes of intently scrutinizing William, the bull turned and walked away in the direction the herd had taken. The first experience of this big-game hunter proved to be somewhat humiliating.

The following morning, after getting some much needed instruction from Jim Crow on how to shoot a buffalo from horseback, William, undaunted, set out on the hunt again. This time a young cow came into his sights, and he brought her down with two shots. He pulled up his horse and found himself completely surrounded by the rushing mass of buffalo set in motion by his charge. Fortunately, the herd separated around him and pounded by, leaving William unscathed. When the captain urged him to kill another, he once again surged into the mass of running beasts. Either William was not fazed by the danger of being trampled that he had just eluded, or his youth knew no fear. This time, his horse ran into a calf and knocked it down. William turned and shot it. He was delighted with having killed two buffalo in twenty minutes. From then on, he was able to provide buffalo to the wagon train as needed for fresh meat. He found buffalo steak cooked on an open fire was "good eating."

When they had passed Pawnee Rock, Kansas, a hunting party of about twenty young Kiowa men joined them. This land was the Natives' hunting grounds. The Kiowas joined the train, riding along and making a general nuisance of themselves. For fun, the young warriors, apparently getting bored, waved their blankets and whooped, stampeding the oxen pulling the wagons. When a wagon master spurred his mule to pursue a wagon, the mule bucked, breaking the cinch on his saddle and throwing the wagon master. The chaos was soon controlled, and the Indians laughed and enjoyed their escapade. There was no way to punish them, because both the Kiowas and Comanches were camped nearby in large numbers.

Some of the Indians arrived at dinnertime with firewood and had to be asked to join the meal. Again, they were quite aggravating. The situation eventually led to the threat of a fight, but tempers were cooled, and the Indians, bored of the sport, finally returned to their camp.

The next morning, soon after getting underway, they came upon the Kiowa camp. It appeared to extend over a square mile and contained the entire tribe—men, women, and children. The curious Indians came pouring out of the camp to inspect these white men and their belongings. About a mile further was the Comanche camp of a similar size. Some of the warriors carried guns, but most had bows and arrows slung on their backs. Little boys, wearing only a breech-clout, had little bows about a foot long and arrows with which they shot targets, like grasshoppers. They were amazingly skilled.

It had been agreed that they would not take a noon break but would continue on as far as possible, to put distance between the wagon train and the curious Indians. However, the Indians persisted in following the wagon train. They raced about, showing off their riding skills and generally having a good time. Eventually the wagon master negotiated with the Indians, trading flour, sugar, and bacon for the Indians' final departure.

Later in the evening, two young Indians galloped into camp, seeking Captain Chiles. The chief had enlisted them to return two blankets that had been stolen by someone in the tribe. The captain rewarded each of them with a cup of sugar, saying that was the first he had ever heard of an Indian returning stolen goods. Indian warriors made their living by raiding other tribes and did not have the same ideas about stealing that white men lived by. In this case, the Indians were respecting the white men's ideas by returning the blankets and, no doubt, wanting to maintain peaceful relations.

With the departure of their pesky guests, the wagon train made good headway to the lower crossing of the Arkansas River, which they would traverse and then head southwest on the Cimarron Route.

The day after they forded the river was the Fourth of July. They celebrated by firing their guns. The captain broke out some jars of gooseberries and ordered pies made to further the festivities. William tells us the gooseberries were okay, but the piecrust was a culinary disaster.

It was warm and dry, and the Cimarron Route was sixty miles of no water between the Arkansas and the Cimarron Rivers. This area was known as the *jornada*—Spanish for dry stretch. To spare animals and men, they started to travel in the late afternoon and continued on through the night. Trekking at night was very quiet. Everyone was weary, and the only sound was that of the rumbling of the wagons and periodic shouts of the drivers.

William rode to the front of the wagons, and by midnight, he was so sleepy he could hardly stay awake. He dismounted and walked with his horse. He tried lying down for a while, but the cacti soon made him realize that was a bad idea. He had great difficulty picking the spines out of his clothes in the dark. He mounted again and rode ahead to where he could no longer hear the wagons. The stars were all that was visible in the darkness. A feeling of melancholy and homesickness seized him. He missed his mother. They were very close. In the solitude and darkness and quiet, he suddenly seemed to realize the danger that was all around him.

With the early light, his forebodings left him and his spirits returned. The young man who charged into the midst of a racing mass of buffalo, without seeming to grasp the possibility of imminent death, must have had a maturing epiphany in the darkness of that empty prairie.

Two days from the Arkansas River at Sand Creek, a tributary of the Cimarron, there was a small pool of stagnant water. It was enough for the men to make coffee in camp but not enough for the oxen. A few hours later, while following the bed of the dry Cimarron, they discovered a small pool of clear water. In this case, the animals didn't wait for the men to drink first. The teams could not be restrained, and they charged with the wagons into the mud to quench their thirst. It required a lot of work to get the wagons unstuck. As they continued following the dry bed of the Cimarron, they would periodically run into other pools of clear, cool water. It was often flavored with alkali but not too bad to the taste. These men and animals were no doubt very thirsty.

One morning it was discovered that Skeesicks was missing, and after a thorough search of the wagons, he remained unfound. Someone reported that he had departed at midnight as one of the guards going out to watch the cattle through the night. When he could not be found, Captain Chiles decided that they could not be delayed for this worthless character, and orders were given for them to move out.

At dinner around the campfire that evening, there was much discussion about whether the train should wait to find the missing man, but the men realized that any opposition to the captain was the same as mutiny and punishable in the same manner.

Then a figure could be seen coming down the road. At first they couldn't tell if it was "a man or a horse or an Indian." The men were very relieved when they recognized Skeesicks. After wandering around for twelve hours without food or water and afraid of attack by wolves, dinner revived the wayward Skeesicks enough to tell his story. As he had left camp to go to the herd, he separated from his guard companion and became totally disoriented. Finally at daylight, he luckily found the road and had sense enough to head west to overtake the wagon train. It was a relief to the men to know they didn't have to abandon a fellow traveler to his fate on the empty prairie.

Ten miles before reaching Fort Union, in current-day New Mexico, they came to a ranch that supplied them with fresh milk and butter. William described the clever design of the adobe spring house. The cold water from the foot of the mountain was re-routed around the spring house so that it ran around tin pans of milk and butter, keeping them fresh. As they were approaching the frontier of settled Spanish ranches, there were often comforts that the uninitiated wouldn't associate with this primitive, far-flung northeastern border of the Territory of New Mexico. In several respects, William's account of the Santa Fe Trail reflected the changes that were occurring, as once-isolated communities benefited from this vibrant trade route. The rancher had a new market for his butter and milk at nearby Fort Union.

At Fort Union, which William found to be neat and clean, in typical military precision, the wagon train split in two. William decided to go with the half that was going to Las Vegas, a thriving town in the Territory. On the way, they arrived at a large adobe ranch house built in the Spanish style, around an inner courtyard. The outer walls had only two openings for entering and exiting. The inner courtyard had openings to provide light and ventilation into the inner rooms. There was a large operation underway, manufacturing buckskin clothes. They were tailored to precision. Again, as they drove deeper into the Territory of New Mexico, there were indications that the frontier was giving way to a settled culture.

They remained in Las Vegas only one day while the wagons were unloaded, and then they reversed their course and headed out on their homeward journey.

Upon arrival at Fort Union, Captain Chiles desired to sell many of their oxen, as the empty wagons on the homebound trip would not require such large teams. He found a buyer for half of the cattle. When the buyer appeared the next morning, he was a well-mounted man on a fine horse and with fine equipment. He had an interesting-looking flask of brandy hanging from his saddle horn. Being a generous man, he proceeded to pass the flask around, and tongue in cheek, William remarked that politeness required taking a good taste of the fine brandy.

When this buyer inquired about hiring some hands to drive the oxen some distance to his home, several men signed on to undertake the task. Then some of the men suggested that the job would be perfect for Skeesicks, who was still hanging around the wagon train. Though Skeesicks was reluctant, he did accept the wages and soon disappeared. William felt sorry for him as he slowly trudged away after the cattle, but it was considered good riddance to see him go. Skeesicks just had not adapted to the rigors of the trail the way his companions had, and he was more of a burden than a help.

With empty wagons, the return trip was going well, until they reached the Arkansas River. There they ran into a company of dragoons that had been fighting all summer against the Cheyenne Indians. In pursuit of the Indians, the troops had marched well ahead of their provision wagons. The soldiers and their horses had undergone a severe campaign; they came around begging for food, tobacco, and whiskey, much like the Indians did. Unfortunately, William's group had little to spare.

The officers warned that it was dangerous to travel in a small group, and they recommended joining other wagon trains that might come along, waiting until they had at least a hundred men and wagons. Captain Chiles decided to wait for several days until a half dozen other trains came up and they could continue more safely in larger numbers.

The wagon-masters of the trains that were behind would come forward and ride with Captain Chiles, William, and others, forming a sociable ride. They had a bit of a scare one day when they observed smoke in a group of trees ahead. Suddenly, about fifty horsemen riding at a fast gallop were coming directly at them. It was hard to tell if they were Indians, but they were galloping in such a pell-mell fashion that Captain Chiles believed they were Indians, because soldiers didn't ride in such a disorderly manner. The captain ordered the formation of a defensive line and they prepared to fight. When the advancing horsemen saw the defensive line they slowed to a walk and continued coming forward until the captain could see that they were the artillery unit attached to the dragoons. They were riding recently captured Cheyenne Indian ponies, which caused the confusion. Anxiety was relieved.

William gave an account of a rare hunting incident that helps us realize that not all the frontiersmen were free of blunders. One day while hunting buffalo, several men topped a hill and saw a herd of about two hundred elk. They immediately took chase and the elk soon scattered. When Captain Chiles, riding William's fast buffalo horse, disappeared ahead, the men followed as fast as they could. They heard shots but were unable to locate Chiles or an elk. All the men, except William and his friend Reece, turned back.

Eventually William and Reece found Chiles and his elk. Chiles had chased this rather fat animal for several miles until it was severely tired. The kill would have been easy, except Chiles's revolvers had not fired properly, and the elk was only wounded slightly. So, finding William's lariat on the saddle, he next managed to lasso the elk, which then turned and rushed Chiles several times, but the experienced hunter continually evaded the charges. He kept following the elk and retrieving his end of the lariat. Eventually, he was able to drive his prey into a narrowing ditch, about ten feet deep, where the elk could not turn around or climb out. The wedge-shaped channel entrapped the tired animal. Once William and Reece arrived, Reece crawled to the edge of the defile and shot the elk, mortally this time. William marveled that Chiles had to be a daredevil to lasso a large bull elk, but Chiles was a stranger to fear.

Now the problem was how to get the elk out of the hole. After withdrawing six miles to camp, they ate dinner and then returned with pack mules and several men to butcher the elk.

Unlike Henry Chatillon (see Chapter 5 - Francis Parkman Jr.), Captain Chiles was not the experienced, measured heroic leader. His youth and personality seem to have led to spontaneous and unexpected exploits and did not make him a good role model. His reputation as a man who had killed several men was again displaying this impulsive quality.

William certainly met his goal of big-game hunting on his trip across the Santa Fe Trail. He managed to avoid the disaster that, as an impulsive youth under the leadership of an equally impulsive youth, could have resulted from some of his hunting endeavors. Few young men had experienced the close calls that he did or had seen the things he saw and survived unscathed. As with the other young men who traveled the trail, hunting the buffalo was almost addictive. Uncle Dick Wootton described it in just such a manner. It seems like the only equally exciting events were fights with the Indians.

When they got within eighty miles of Westport, William joined a forced ride with Captain Chiles to arrive at Westport before the wagons. It was late September, and rest in a comfortable bed with a roof overhead was a welcome luxury. He never discussed any difficulties with his health on the trip, and he seemed to thrive. The Santa Fe Trail led many to a life in the West and was a road to the development of the country, but it also proved to afford some young men an opportunity for growing up and learning.

11

JOSÉ LIBRADO GURULÉ
ON THE TRAIL OF NECESSITY

COMPARED TO THE OREGON Trail, upon which many immigrants traveled West and kept a record of their experiences, the Santa Fe Trail had very few journals or memoirs left behind. Because most of the travelers to the Southwest were illiterate or simply conducting business, they did not chronicle their experiences. Moreover, of the accounts we do have, most were written by Americans.

Unfortunately, from the hundreds of Hispanic men who labored on the trail, few stories survive. However, the story of José Gurulé, though short, does give us an amazing picture of what it was like to work on a Mexican wagon train traveling East to trade and returning to New Mexico. As an older man, José told his story, and it appears in the book, *When We Were Young in the West*, by Richard Melzer, PhD.

José was a descendant of one of the families who first settled the village of Las Placitas, New Mexico, in the mid-eighteenth century. The town was part of a Spanish land grant, and as such, the wealth in the area was centralized and controlled by one person. By 1867, José's family was living in poverty and, like the other families of the village, was in debt to the wealthy landowner, José Leander Perea, of Bernalillo, north of Albuquerque. It was as though the men of the village had become serfs, because they had to serve the patrón to try to pay off what they owed.

Each spring, as it neared the time when the Spanish caravans would head east with their loads of sheep's wool to sell in the United States, the captain of the patrón's freight operation arrived in the village. He came to select the strongest of the men to work on the wagon caravan. In February 1867, when José was sixteen, he was chosen, along with his father, to make the trip. The captain was experienced at selecting men of endurance for this arduous work.

The men had to provide a suit of clothing that would last for three months, along with a pair of shoes or moccasins. Their bedroll was a serape (shawl) or blanket woven on the village looms.

At José Perea's home, the cookhouse was busy preparing food for the men while they traveled. Dried peas were ground between stones for "coffee." Hundreds of tortillas were made. Mutton and goat meat was dried. Beans, onions, black-eyed peas, and chilies were packed. A rolling commissary dispensed food to the men daily. Each man carried his own cube sugar and tobacco.

Ten laden wagons, each pulled by five pairs of oxen, departed Las Placitas for Las Vegas, where they would join up to form a caravan of about four hundred wagons. There was also a large herd of mules and oxen to replace those that fell along the way.

Wagons carried feed for the animals, water, the commissary, and firewood, along with the loads of wool.

Each man carried a small gourd of water to drink as he walked. At each watering hole, the gourd was refilled.

They set out about the middle of February, with the prayers of those left behind petitioning for the safety of their men and boys. From the beginning of the trip, a demanding schedule was set that pushed men and animals to the limit. They were required to roll eighteen hours a day. Driving through the night, they halted about ten in the morning. Animals were unharnessed, food was quickly eaten, and the men got some sleep. When the animals were turned out, they almost collapsed with exhaustion. In six hours, the caravan was rolling again.

Campsites for the six-hour stop were selected in open spaces where the ground was barren, so no fires would menace them. This also helped avoid Indians starting fires to thwart their advance. Sometimes to make the campsite in the right place at the right time, the men had to run and goad the oxen to travel fast.

Men received a full meal once a day, and twice a day they got a snack of an onion and a tortilla. It was a schedule to kill any man or boy who didn't have great strength and endurance.

One day, a heavily loaded wagon was brought to a tipped angle by its oxen, causing the train to stop suddenly. A man had fallen asleep on the tongue of one of the wagons, and he fell off and was trampled. There was a short stop to bury him. This kind of accident happened all too often with exhausted men.

Another day, as they approached the crossing of the Arkansas River, a large band of Indians was sighted on the horizon, advancing toward the wagons. The order went out to hold fire, but someone fired at the Indians as they neared. The fire was returned, and a man with the wagons went down. Luckily, before full-scale war broke out, the captain was able to make signs of friendship to the Indians, and the situation was defused. The wagon train had no horses, so the Indians were much less tempted to cause trouble, because there was nothing they wanted. Another deterrent that day was that this was a tribal camp on the move. When warriors were traveling with women and children, as they were this day, they avoided fighting situations—unlike war parties, which never included women and children.

One old woman got off her travois and approached José and indicated a desire for some sugar he had. He gave her some, and she thanked him in a language he could not understand—at least, he assumed it was thanks that she said. She then went to her pack and retrieved some meat to offer to José, and he thanked her in Spanish. Then she returned to her horse and the whole band soon disappeared from sight.

In three months, the caravan rolled into Kansas City, Missouri. Now the men were kept busy unloading the wagons, hauling their wares to storage, and preparing their animals for the return trip.

Occasionally, the men had some time to wander around, seeking colorful and interesting sights. They were amused to see on a building a large picture of a man they believed was Tomasita, the Indian leader from the Pueblo Revolt in Taos in 1847 against Governor Charles Bent and the American occupation. They were surprised that Tomasita was known this far away. No one knew why the picture was there.

As they strolled on, they heard music and encountered a Negro band playing outside a minstrel show. They had no money to attend the show, but they listened from outside. José had sold some of his goats before leaving home, so he could buy a worsted suit from a store. He would not break his promise to himself by spending his money elsewhere.

Their stay in Kansas City was short, and soon they were headed west again. The wagons were heavily loaded now with all kinds of merchandise for the Perea store in Bernalillo. On the trip back, they saw very few buffalo, and only one was within rifle range. A member of the train shot at that buffalo and it went down. The shooter ran to him and jumped on him to start butchering, but to his great surprise the buffalo jumped up. There was nothing to do but grab onto the animal's long hair and take the ride of a lifetime. He got about a twenty-minute, thousand-yard ride before the rifle bullet finally weakened the buffalo and he went down to stay. They had fresh meat that night and a story to tell— at least that was the story told by José!

And then cholera hit the caravan. When a man fell ill, he was put into a wagon and those remaining on their feet had to manage driving the oxen. Eventually, so many were sick that they stopped at a spring to doctor the men. The only medicine they had was plenty of whiskey with chili in it. After twelve days, they went on with a bare skeleton crew of men. Whiskey and chili had not cured anyone. They had to make frequent stops, and many men died. Mounds of dirt were the only markers for their graves.

It was December when they finally reached Bernalillo. A third of the men had not made it, and the survivors were a very exhausted bunch. For their eleven months of labor and danger, each man received eight dollars. It is not known if the families of those who died received any payments. The rejoicing and celebrating for the safe return of the men from Placitas helped make up for the lack of dollars. None of the Placitas men had gotten cholera. José was a young man of seventeen when he arrived home. To great admiration, he proudly wore the first store-bought suit of clothes ever seen in the village.

We don't know anything of José's life after his trip on the Santa Fe Trail, except that he was eighty-eight years old in 1940, when he related his story and it was recorded. Thanks to the New Mexico Federal Writers Project, he was able to share his vivid memories of travel on the Santa Fe Trail as a young man. It is a short story of what it was like to travel as a hard-working laborer going west to east in 1867.

José's story and those of many of his fellow New Mexicans, like the stories of the Indians who saw the Santa Fe Trail leading to disaster, are important to know. They remind us there are many perspectives on the changes this great route of trade brought. The Santa Fe Trail will always be an important part of our history, not only for being the road of westward expansion but also because its stories connect us to these travelers of the past.

José's story was a story of travel dictated by necessity. We will never know how many stories of necessity similar to this one were simply never recorded.

12

CONCLUSION
ON THE TRAIL TO HISTORY

CHRISTOPHER "KIT" CARSON, JOSIAH Gregg, Richens Lacy "Uncle Dick" Wootton, Francis Parkman Jr., Susan Shelby Magoffin, Hector Lewis Garrard, Marion Sloan Russell, James Ross Larkin, William B. Napton, and José Librado Gurulé are names of young people who were not afraid to travel into an unknown wilderness, with all its inherent dangers. They were in their teens and early twenties when they left behind security to undertake the trip of a lifetime. How many of us today would do that? How many have such an opportunity? What an advantage it is to have their stories to learn from and to help us to understand our own lives.

The American frontier is no longer a geographical location. Today's frontiers include research in medicine, space, or environmental change. Yet our world was shaped by those earlier pioneers; they are our predecessors and our teachers, helping us through their examples to nurture the same qualities of courage, perseverance, and resourcefulness. Like them, we can aspire to overcome any obstacles to building a safe, productive, and satisfying life for ourselves. Like them, we are pioneers of a future yet to come.

Each generation has opportunities and challenges that are unique. The Santa Fe Trail of the nineteenth century offered experiences of freedom that are no longer options today. To ride a horse now from Independence, Missouri, to Santa Fe, New Mexico, would certainly be nearly impossible because of fences, highways, and buildings. We can only imagine what it was like to experience the beauty of the open prairie and to suffer the hardships of horseback travel in the open. But we can envy that opportunity, feel the loss of it, and try to live up to the values of people who did it.

Even when we take into account the racial prejudices of that era and the destructiveness of Manifest Destiny to the native populations, we can appreciate the amazing beauty and opportunity this land offered. We can criticize the course that others took and at the same time understand, from their perspective, what their time called on them to do. The wonder of history is the offering of understanding and lessons we can try to build on. We are our past.

BIBLIOGRAPHY

Alexander, Eveline M. *Cavalry Wife: The Diary of Eveline M. Alexander, 1866–1867.* Edited by Sandra L. Myres. College Station: Texas A&M University Press, 1977.

Brewerton, George Douglas. *Overland with Kit Carson: A Narrative of the Old Spanish Trail in '48.* Lincoln: University of Nebraska Press, 1993.

Carter, Harvey Lewis. *"Dear Old Kit": The Historical Christopher Carson.* Norman: University of Oklahoma Press, 1990.

Conard, Howard L. *"Uncle Dick" Wootton: The Pioneer Frontiersman of the Rocky Mountain Region.* Chicago: W. E. Dibble & Co., 1890. Reprinted 1980 from the 1890 edition.

Duffus, R. L. *The Santa Fe Trail.* Albuquerque: First University of New Mexico Press, 1972.

Garrard, Lewis H. *Wah-to-yah and the Taos Trail.* Norman: University of Oklahoma Press, 1955.

Gregg, Josiah. *Commerce of the Prairies; or, The Journal of a Santa Fe Trader during Eight Expeditions.* Philadelphia: J. W. Moore, 1851. Reprinted from the 1851 edition by Applewood Books (Carlisle MA).

Larkin, James Ross. *Reluctant Frontiersman: James Ross Larkin on the Santa Fe Trail, 1856–57.* Edited by Barton

H. Barbour. Albuquerque: University of New Mexico Press, 1990.

Marcy, Randolph Barnes. *Thirty Years of Army Life on the Border. 1866.* Facsimile of the first edition by Harper & Brothers, NY. Internet: http://RareBooksClub.com, 2013.

Magoffin, Susan Shelby. *Down the Santa Fe Trail and into Mexico: The Diary of Susan Shelby Magoffin, 1846–1847.* Lincoln: University of Nebraska Press, 1982.

Melzer, Richard. *When We Were Young in the West: True Stories of Childhood.* Santa Fe: Sunstone Press, 2003.

Napton, William B. *Over the Santa Fe Trail, 1857.* Kansas City: Franklin Hudson Publishing Co., 1905. Reprinted online by Leopold Classic Library, www.leopoldclassiclibrary.com.

Parkman, Francis Jr. *The Oregon Trail.* New York: Penguin Classics, 1985.

Quaife, Milo Milton, ed. *Kit Carson's Autobiography.* By Kit Carson. Lincoln: University of Nebraska Press, 1966. First published 1935 by Bison Book.

Remley, David. *Kit Carson: The Life of an American Border Man.* Norman: University of Oklahoma Press, 2012.

Russell, Marion Sloan, as dictated to Mrs. Hal Russell. *Land of Enchantment: Memoirs of Marion Russell along the Santa Fe Trail.* Albuquerque: University of New Mexico Press, 1981.

Sabin, Edwin L. *Kit Carson Days, 1809–1868.* 2 vols. Lincoln: University of Nebraska Press, 1995.

Sides, Hampton. *Blood and Thunder*. New York: Anchor Books, October 2007.

Simmons, Marc. *Kit Carson & His Three Wives*. Albuquerque: University of New Mexico Press, 2003.

ACKNOWLEDGMENTS

Thanks to my family—Mom and daughters Chris and Trish, who always encouraged me to stick to this seemingly endless project. They never suggested that I should give up something that might never be fulfilled or lucrative.

Thanks to book developer Lora Lisbon, who started me down the thorny path of book proposals and finding an editor, and for making me think this was actually possible.

Thanks to my editor Mary Neighbour, of Media-Neighbours. She always kept me on the path to perfection and has become a wonderful friend. Without her, this book would never have been.

Thanks to Leo Oliva for all his amazing help. He has researched and written about the Santa Fe Trail for fifty years and has been the editor of the Santa Fe Trail Association quarterly, *Wagon Tracks*, for twenty-five years. I think of him as a giving mentor and born teacher.

A big thanks goes to Mr. Marc Simmons, renowned historian of the Southwest and the Santa Fe Trail. When he agreed to read from the manuscript and then gave me a warm endorsement, I felt his opinion would give me a "go" or "no go" view of my manuscript. I have unending respect for his knowledge of the subject.

THE AUTHOR

©*Orlando Diaz*

Camilla "Cam" Kattell has been an airplane pilot, a stockbroker, and horsewoman.

Now that she is retired, she is pursuing her dream to write and following her passion for history. Cam's pride and joy are her two grown daughters, a son-in-law, two grandsons, and her 96-year-old mother.

Cam lives in New Mexico.

CPSIA information can be obtained
at www.ICGtesting.com
Printed in the USA
FSOW01n2330051015
11777FS